Ben F. Williams, Jr.'s

TALES OF MY SOUTHWEST

Ben F Williams Jr
2007

Ben F. Williams, Jr.'s

TALES OF MY SOUTHWEST

Smokin Z Press Tucson, Arizona

To contact the author or order
additional copies of this book
write to us at:
P.O. Box 13121
Tucson, Arizona 85732
or email us at:
bfw@smokin-z.com
or visit the web site:
www.smokin-z.com

This edition was prepared for printing by
Ghost River Images
5350 East Fourth Street
Tucson, Arizona 85711
ghostriverimages.com

Cover design by Cornelia Kazal

ISBN-13: 978-0-9794800-0-3
ISBN-10: 0-9794800-0-0
Library of Congress Control Number: 2007933782

Printed in the United States of America

Second Printing: October, 2007
10 9 8 7 6 5 4 3 2 1

Contents

dedicated to Daisy --- my Little Flower --- with love

Ben

ARIZONA
NEW MEXICO
TEXAS
Duncan
Roswell
Rio Grande
Phoenix
WILLOW SPRINGS RANCH
Lordsburg
Las Cruces
Willcox
Tucson
Deming
Benson
Tombstone
Rodeo
Columbus
El Paso
Bisbee
RANCHO LAS PALMAS
Ciudad Juarez
Ft. Huachuca
Nogales
Douglas
SAN BERNARDINO RANCH
LAS PALOMAS RANCH
Nogales
Naco
Agua Prieta
PALOMAS RANCH HQ
Ascencion
Cananea
Jenoverachi
Fronteras
ANGOSTURA LAKE
AJOS RANCH
Janos
Magdalena
Bacoachi
Nacozari
GUADALUPE MINE
Bavispe
SANTA ROSA RANCH
Colonia Dublan
Arispe
LAKE NOVILLO
Cumpas
Casas Grandes
Divisaderos
San Pedro de la Cueva
Batuc
Hermosillo
LA GLORIA MINE
SONORA
CHIHUAHUA
MEXICO
NOT TO SCALE

ACKNOWLEDGMENTS

A great number of people have urged, prodded and assisted me in my writing. To mention a few, but by no means all, and at the risk of offending by way of omission someone who has been instrumental in my efforts, I wish to thank my wife, Daisy, and my children – Liz Boyd, Diane Belcher, Katie Braun and Ben III – for having been excellent sounding boards and critics, as well as editors from time to time.

Kate McMillan, a colleague, originally suggested that I take writing classes from Pima Community College upon my retirement from law practice, which I did, and in so doing met Meg Park and Sam Turner, two excellent instructors in memoir writing.

Stories have been pent up within me for many years. Meg and Sam opened the door and stories started to spill out from pen to paper. Jamie and George Metanovich and Esther Capin continually urged me to tell my stories in writing. Pat Lo Biondo helped transcribe a few of my first stories, while Marilyn Bender got with the program. Through her skills of typing, layout and organization, we were able to write stories that were technically acceptable. I thank Elizabeth Ohm, Maurine Kish and Dixie Nixon for their invaluable assistance in proofreading my stories. Roberto Ruiz, Bob McCartan and Albert Kazal, Jr. gave me good ideas and encouragement. Sheila Bender's incredible experience and sound ideas were useful.

A writing group known as "Quail Run" provided helpful ideas for effective written expression. Sam Turner, Penny Porter, Bev Malnar, Bobbie Schlesinger, Flo Marks, Ann Deslauriers, Sharon Landeen and Ruth Beach are in that group. Penny Porter was a sagacious mentor. Nan Ames of the Douglas Historical Society and Chrystal Burke of the Arizona Historical Society have been particularly helpful. Corlyn Holbrook Adams was generous in providing old letters and documents about Bateman Wilhelm, my great-grandfather and Marion Williams, my grandfather.

Several of my stories have appeared in the *Tombstone Epitaph National Edition*, *Range Magazine* and *Precision Shooting Magazine*.

A number of friends and 78 years of incredible life experiences provided the inspiration and ideas for the stories you are about to read.

Enjoy!

FOREWORD

by

Governor Raúl H. Castro

Tales of My Southwest is recommended reading for everyone. The book is a narration of life in the southeastern part of Arizona, southwest New Mexico and the northern states of Sonora and Chihuahua, Mexico. It is informative as well as entertaining.

I can vouch for the authenticity of the way of life as described in the book. I personally know most of those areas, and ranching and mining were not foreign to me while I resided on the Arizona-New Mexico border.

The author is truly a third-generation Arizonan. I will soon be 91 years of age, and it so happens that I met the author's grandfather, Marion Williams, in Douglas, Arizona – except that when I met him, he was generally referred to as "Don Mariano." The word "Don" before his name is a symbol of respect. He was well-known in all the Arizona-Sonora border communities.

During the early 1920s, I was employed in the American Consulate at Agua Prieta, Sonora, Mexico. It was at that time that I met the author's father, Ben F. Williams, Sr. He was prominent in the Douglas-Agua Prieta communities and was a successful cattle rancher, miner and businessman. He took me under his wing and was forever explaining how things were done in Mexico. I was always happy to accept his fatherly advice. As the years passed, I have had the good fortune of meeting most of the Williams family.

As I read the book, I was overtaken by a siege of nostalgia, as the persons mentioned are all personally known to me. The geographical areas mentioned are also well-known to me. Much space in the book is given to mining events in Cananea, Sonora, Mexico. I was born in Cananea, where my father, Francisco D. Castro, was a leader in the continued existence of the mining union known as *Sindicato 65*. In fact, during my father's regime, there was a miners' strike which the Mexican government declared to be a "wildcat strike." As a consequence, my father was incarcerated in Hermosillo. He was later cleared, however, and the end result was that the Castro family was permitted to enter the United States to reside in Pirtleville, Arizona.

It's a small world, for as years passed and I became an attorney, I was engaged as Bill Greene's lawyer. He was the son of Colonel Greene, founder of the mining and smelter operations in Cananea.

Because of my work in the American Consulate at Agua Prieta, Sonora, I had the good fortune of meeting most of the area's major cattle ranchers, mining entrepreneurs and businessmen. Frequently during roundup time, the cattle ranchers would invite me to join them and I would usually accept, as I loved the action.

At the time when I was working for the U.S. consulate in Agua Prieta, I was not well-acquainted with the author, for he is much younger than I. Later on in my career, when I became a Superior Court judge in Pima County, Arizona, I would from time to time preside over the court in Bisbee. By that time, Ben, Jr., had become well-known and had a reputation as a very capable attorney. He has now retired from the practice of law, and he and his charming wife, Daisy, have moved from Douglas to Tucson, Arizona. We keep in touch with them regularly, and I consider Ben a truly close friend.

Raúl H. Castro
Former Governor, State of Arizona
April 30, 2007

PREFACE

Faced with retirement after 50 years of law practice, I pondered what I might do to occupy my time. The urge to write had been pent up in me for years, and only when I enrolled in creative memoir writing classes did this urge surge into reality. The key in the lock was turned, and the door to my stored-up tales opened. I began writing.

My purpose in creating this work is twofold: First, to chronicle and preserve experiences as I have found them in my life or as have been related to me, and second, to write a collection of short stories, hopefully with sufficient humor to be of interest to all readers.

Granddad, Marion L. Williams

MARION LEE WILLIAMS – 1871

Marion Lee Williams was born on December 15, 1871, in Long Valley, Utah, to Grace Tippet Jose (date of birth July 14, 1842) of Lanner, Cornwall County, England, and Bateman Haight Wilhelm (sometimes known as Bateman Williams) of Venice, New York (date of birth November 14, 1844).

Grace and Bateman were married on August 2, 1870, by Apostle Joseph F. Smith of the Mormon Church in Salt Lake City, Utah. It was the second marriage for Bateman, a polygamist, and Grace, a divorcee. Bateman founded Erastus, a small farming settlement, after which they lived in Concho, Arizona Territory, 16 miles west of St. Johns, for 14 years.

In 1884, Bateman and six other men were indicted by an Arizona Territorial grand jury, charged with the crime of polygamy: William J. Flake, Peter J. Christofferson, C.I. Kemp, Ammon Tenney, James N. Scouson and D.K. Udall. When Bateman learned of the jury's indictment, he fled to Mexico, leaving in the middle of the night in August, 1884, later sending for Grace and their children.

The family lived in Jenoverachi, Sonora, south of Cananea, for several years, making a meager living farming, after which they moved to Tombstone, Arizona Territory, in the late 1880s.

Marion had five sisters: Independence ("Pen"), Mary, Lucy, Amelia and Frances. He was a short man, just 5'7" tall, with flaming red hair, a red moustache, and steel-blue eyes. He wore size-seven shoes.

Marion's father, Bateman, liked to drink, and on a number of occasions, abused Marion's dearly-beloved mother. Marion had an innate knowledge of human nature and a keen sense of the rights of others. One night, Bateman came home drunk and began beating Grace. Running out into the yard, Marion grabbed a singletree from a wagon, returned to the house and hit his father over the head, knocking him cold. This ended Marion's residency in the home. Marion was 14 at the time.

Leaving home, Marion applied for a job at the Oso Negro (black bear) Mine 16 miles southwest of Nacozari, Sonora. Jim Kirk, mining engineer and part owner of the mine, took a liking to Marion and put him to work sorting for the richest ore, or, as the miners say, "high-grading."

Small of stature, he was not able to do heavy work at first. As he grew older and stronger, he was put to work driving an ore car out of the mine. Later, he became a mule skinner, driving an 18-mule ore wagon from the mine to the Cananea Consolidated Mining Company smelter.

Granddad when he was a young man.
Photo courtesy of Corlyn Holbrook Adams

While living in Tombstone, Marion was befriended by John Slaughter, the sheriff famous for bringing law and order to Cochise County. Slaughter offered him an opportunity to get an education: "Marion, if you'll take care of the chores around my home, feed the chickens, milk the cow and look after the livestock, I'll see to it that you go to school and get an education."

"Thank you kindly for your offer, Mr. Slaughter, but I do not want to be beholden to any man."

Thus, Marion's book education was

Granddad's five sisters.
Photo courtesy of Corlyn Holbrook Adams

limited to that which he received as a young man of 20, when, at the suggestion of his mentor, Jim Kirk (who had roots there), he went to Beloit, Kansas, where he received only a year's worth of rudimentary schooling.

Returning to Bacoachi, Sonora, Marion, age 24, and Teresa del Rio, a comely young woman of 20, were married. They built a house on his Ajos Ranch, where they began their family of 11 children, only five of whom survived – Ella, Ben, Eva, Dell and Annamae. Grace, Leo M., Emma, Marion Lee, Jr., and another son named Leo all died from typhoid or dyptheria.

Granddad – Marion Lee Williams – had a marvelous sense of humor and loved to tell stories, as do I.

SILENT PARTNER – 1894

In 1894, Marion Williams, 23, was living on a ranch at Jenoverachi, Sonora, Mexico, 10 miles east of Cananea, 84 miles south of Naco, Arizona Territory. His beloved sister, Frances, and brother-in-law, Charlie Holbrook, lived nearby. They made a meager living farming, had two children and were expecting their third child when Charlie "up and died."

Frances asked her brother, Marion, my grandfather, to find a way to take Charlie's body to Tombstone, Arizona Territory, for burial. "Please," she begged. "You know Charlie didn't want to be buried in Mexico. He wanted to go home."

"Frances, you know bodies cannot be taken out of Mexico. But I know how much you want him to be buried at home, so I'll do my darndest to find a way."

"How are you going to do it?"

"Don't worry, dear sister. Just bring me Charlie's best clothes and a hat."

Marion dressed Charlie in his very best clothes and put the hat on his head. He then wrapped Charlie's fully-clothed body in a serape, a colorful, handwoven Mexican blanket. With Frances' help, he lifted Charlie into the front seat of the buckboard, a horse or mule-drawn buggy with springs used for comfortable traveling.

As Granddad and his upright, but deceased, traveling companion approached the international border at Naco, he was greeted by Mexican customs officials. They knew him well because, having lived in Jenoverachi for many years, he crossed often.

"*Buenos dias, Don Mariano. A donde vas tan apurado?*" (Good morning, Don Mariano. Where are you going in such a hurry?)

"*Voy a Tombstone con mi cuñado. Está muy enfermo.* " (I am going to Tombstone with my brother-in-law. He's very sick.)

"What's the matter with him?" they asked.

"He has smallpox."

The palaver ceased and they waved him through.

Pase. Pase pronto. No pare. Sáquelo de aqui!" (Pass. Don't stop. Go quickly. Get him out of here.)

Granddad popped his whip, and the horses and buckboard and his silent partner vanished in a cloud of dust on their way to Tombstone.

Arrangements were made, and Charlie Holbrook was laid to rest in Plot 3, Row 25, Section A, of the Tombstone Cemetery, where he "remains" to this day.

"PEG LEG" FINNEY – 1898

It was September 18, 1898, when Granddad rode horseback from his ranch near Jenoverachi, Mexico, to Naco, Arizona, on business. He left his horse and favorite saddle at the livery stable for the night.

When Granddad went to get his horse and saddle early the next morning, Jake, the stable owner, said, "Marion, I've got bad news."

"What's that?"

"Someone stole a horse and saddle last night. I'm sorry, but the saddle was yours. I've reported the theft to Judge Starr Williams at the courthouse in Bisbee."

"Well, I'll be damned. I've got to ride back to the ranch today. Do you have a saddle I can rent or borrow?"

"Sorry, Marion, I sure wish I could help, but I don't have an extra saddle."

Granddad rode back to the ranch in great discomfort, sorely missing his skillfully handcrafted, fine leather Gallup-Frazier saddle.

Cochise County Sheriff, John Slaughter, lived at his San Bernardino Ranch 15 miles east of Douglas. In order to maintain communication with the courthouse in Bisbee, a telephone wire was strung on steel poles, for a distance of at least 37 miles. It remained in service for more than 40 years until Granddad purchased the ranch from Mrs. Slaughter.

Sometime during mid-morning on September 19th, Sheriff Slaughter received a telephone call from Judge Williams in Bisbee. "Thought you ought to know, Sheriff, Arthur 'Peg Leg' Finney stole a horse and Marion Williams' saddle during the night. It's been reported that he's riding east toward El Paso."

(Finney, who shined shoes around Bisbee and Naco, was a known thief and troublemaker.)

The next day, on September 20th, word was sent to Granddad informing him that a saddle had been recovered. He would need to go to the sheriff's office in Bisbee to identify it.

Granddad rode into Bisbee, arriving as the wagon pulled in from the San Bernardino Ranch.

Deputy Sam Miller, a friend of Granddad's, greeted him. "Hello, Marion. How's it going?"

"Mostly by bareback," he groaned. "Do you have my saddle?"

"Describe it."

"A Gallup-Frazier with a broken saddle string," he said without hesitation.

"It's yours. Take it."

"Thanks, and be sure to give my thanks to Sheriff Slaughter."

It seems that Peg Leg was seen at the Slaughter Ranch on the 19th, and when Sheriff Slaughter and two deputies went to arrest him, a gunfight ensued. Finney was shot and killed and Granddad's saddle was recovered.

Arthur "Peg Leg" Finney was buried in the cemetery at the Slaughter Ranch on September 20th, where he rests in peace to this day.

The inquest into the killing of Arthur Finney, alias Peg Leg, was filed in the District Court, First Judicial District, County of Cochise, Territory of Arizona, on September 28, 1898.

THE SPARK THAT STARTED THE MEXICAN REVOLUTION - 1906

May 18, 2006, marked the 100th anniversary of the devastating San Francisco earthquake, a natural catastrophe that will live in history forever.

June 6, 1906, marked the anniversary of the Cananea-Sonora riots that touched the lives of many in southern Arizona and northern Mexico, including Marion Williams.

A busy but unhappy town, Cananea, lying 50 miles south of Tombstone, Arizona Territory, was a large copper mining camp with mines and smelters going full blast, and more than 2,500 employees. The workers were paid three pesos or $1.50 a day for ten hours work by Colonel W. Greene's mining company. They wanted more pay and shorter hours.

Marion Williams was born in Utah Territory in 1871, and had come to the Cananea area with his parents in the late 1880s. He had great natural intellect, but little book learning. He could write, but his words were mostly phonetic, not the King's English. Two decades after his arrival in Cananea, Marion bought the Santa Rosa Ranch 10 miles outside the town. His business partner in the ranch was Frank Bishop, a San Francisco lawyer.

Hearing of the earthquake, Marion was concerned for Frank, as he was a good friend as well as his partner. However, another historic event was to personally touch his life 19 days later.

Riding into Cananea the day before the strike, Marion went to visit his friend, Jim Kirk, mine superintendent and assistant to Colonel Greene.

"There's going to be trouble, Marion. Union agitators have the workers stirred up into a mean mood. Don't get involved in this...you could lose your ranch and your family. Let the company handle it."

Dr. Phillipe Barroso, Mayor of Cananea, stayed up all night attempting to find out what the miners and their leaders were planning. Pablo Rubio, *comisario* (justice of the peace), telephoned the mayor at 5 a.m. "The strike is on! You and I need to make a personal inspection. Perhaps our presence and influence will accomplish some good."

The two men picked up Arturo Carrillo, the judge at Ronquillo, a part of the Cananea complex, and drove to Oversight, the mine headquarters.

Nearly 400 chanting miners greeted them, demanding more pay for shorter hours, and shouting, "Viva Mexico." The mayor and two judges prevailed on the unhappy miners, asking them to select a group of 14 to represent them at a meeting Mayor Barroso promised to arrange.

At the conference, the miners requested the following: a pay raise from three to five pesos a day; all workers to be paid more than the minimum of three pesos; the hours reduced from ten to eight per day; that promotions be left open for qualified Mexicans within the company to advance; and that half of the foremen be Mexicans. They further complained of being required to trade at company stores where prices were always higher.

The 14-member delegation prepared and submitted to Colonel Greene, the president of Greene Cananea Copper Company, the following statement of their dissatisfaction:

"We the undersigned delegates designated by the Mexican miners to present our case to you, make this statement: That although injurious to our own interest and to our personal dignity, we have served the company over which you preside, although none of us has been pleased by, or found any basis in equity for, the pay offered to Mexicans."

At the time, Americans were paid $5.00 a day while Mexicans earned only $1.50, an aggravating "bur under their saddle blankets."

Three Mexican officials were selected to meet with the committee of 14 representatives: Barroso, Pablo Rubio and Pedro Robles, the company lawyer, to explain the company's attitudes and Mexican laws applicable to the situation. It was hoped the three Mexicans could handle the situation better because of the rising anger against Americans.

At ten o'clock on the morning of June 1, 1906, Barroso, Rubio and Robles met the strikers behind closed doors, while outside some 2,000 striking miners had gathered to await the results. There were chants of, "*Ocho horas, cinco pesos*" (eight hours, five pesos).

Handbills were circulated in Spanish which said, among other things:

> "PEOPLE arouse yourselves and ACT. LEARN that which you seem to have forgotten. Congregate and discuss your rights. DEMAND the respect that is due you.
>
> Every Mexican whom the foreigner despised is worth just as much as, or more than, those foreigners, if he will join with his brothers and CLAIM his rights.
>
> CURSE the thoughts that a Mexican is worth less than a Yankee; that a Negro or Chinaman is to be compared with a Mexican. That this is a fact is the result of a very bad government which gives the advantages to adventurers rather than to the true owners of this unfortunate land. MEXICANS, AWAKEN! The country and your dignity demand it!
>
> Cananea, June 1, 1906."

Colonel Greene, who was popular among the miners, came to address them and explained that a blanket raise of a peso per person would be risky for the company in view of the great number of men employed and further, the hours expected of the workers depended on the job. As for the charge that everybody had to pay higher prices at the company store, he assured them that the prices of necessities were constantly being reduced and were, in 1906, thirty-percent lower than they had been two years before, and much lower than at any other mine in Mexico. He urged them to work together to make Cananea the most important mining town in Mexico and to get rid of all "adventurers without conscience" whose intrigues were injuring the community.

Porfirio Diaz, dictator of Mexico for thirty years who had ruled with an iron hand, was nearing the end of his supremacy. He wanted Mexico to be a great modern nation, but he favored the affluent – his friends and supporters – while the lives of the rest were likened to those of slaves.

The miners' union, an American organization, Western Federation of Miners, had unionized thousands of mine workers in both countries. The Mexican liberals and the Federation of Miners were interested in promoting discontent among miners in Mexico, and their agents were alive and well and active in Cananea. They had help on the local Cananea level from Enrique Bermúdez, a young Mexican journalist who lived for a short time in Douglas. He published a radical newspaper called *"El Centenario"* and moved the publication from Douglas to Cananea in April of 1906, further pouring fuel on already hot coals. His publication had been circulating for some time among a small group of miners and office workers, who were already organized prior to the June 6 crisis.

Colonel Greene and his people were aware of what was going on, for in one of his reports, Greene said, "I was informed by a man working in the *Cobre Grande*, one of the mines in the complex, that agitators of the Western Federation had been through the mines, inciting the Mexicans, and had furnished money for the socialist club established in Cananea."

The Western Federation planned, according to the reports coming to Colonel Greene, to "dynamite the bank," where it was believed the company had one million dollars, and to "break open the store and get firearms and ammunition, and with them, start a revolution against the government of Porfirio."

Management at the mine ignored this information until they learned that several boxes of dynamite were reported missing from the Oversight, where the leaders of the liberal club worked.

During the night Colonel Greene received word of the strike. He ordered a Pullman car and locomotive to take him to Bisbee to arrange for reinforcements and pick up all the firearms he could lay his hands on. He went directly to W. H. Brophy's Copper Queen store, which had been kept open in response to Greene's telephone message. Greene collected every gun in the place – 98 rifles and 20 pistols, along with 5,000 rounds of ammunition. When he returned at four in the morning, he distributed the arms to 40 of his "most reliable men" and waited out the night in his home.

Around eleven o'clock in the morning, Colonel Greene came down from his home, which was located on the mesa overlooking town. He was tired, having been up most of the night. He did not seem disturbed when he spoke to the miners; in fact, he remained calm even when the trouble was at its worst.

The tension rose as he began to walk among the onlookers and bystanders, shaking hands with them here and there and advising the men not to let themselves be deceived by troublemakers. He reminded the crowd that the company paid higher wages than any mining firm in Mexico, which was true; that he had always looked out for them and their welfare, which was really the point at issue; and that he wished to treat them like men and would listen to reasonable requests, but he had to follow government regulations. And finally, he suggested they ought to go home.

They listened to the colonel, and as he left, they cheered him with "*Viva el Coronel Greene*."

After Colonel Greene returned to his home, most of the miners left, but a small core remained and their mood changed. They felt the company had made no concessions; Barroso explained that no concessions were possible. The Mexican government had ordered not only that wages must be kept down, but they must be reduced. Too many men were coming to the camp looking for work at three pesos a day – several times what they could earn at ranch or farm work – and employers had raised such a fuss that Governor Izabál had stepped in. In other words, the company's "hands were tied."

The organizers laughed at this expression and told the men, "This is no answer. Greene is making excuses and must be taught a lesson. The strike will go on! Injustice and discrimination must stop!"

"Why should a Mexican workman be paid three pesos or $1.50 American a day for ten hours work, when an American gets $5 a day? Do the American invaders own Mexico? Posterity will remember you for what you are about to do. Every worker must walk off his job...everybody! Now!"

At two o'clock that afternoon the large crowd was back on the main street, and they had a plan: They would visit every unit and make sure all work stopped.

The march began. They moved toward the mesa. They were determined, but not hostile, yet. There was no stopping until they reached the company lumber yard at the extreme eastern end of the mesa.

At the lumber yard, things grew worse. The lumber yard was managed by the two Metcalf brothers, one of whom turned a high-pressure water hose on the crowd, infuriating the strikers. George and his brother were killed, stabbed repeatedly with miners' "candlesticks," the sharp, stiletto-like devices used to hold candles in the rock walls of underground tunnels.

After killing the Metcalfs and setting fire to the lumber yard, the strikers proceeded up the mesa toward Greene's house. Having seen the smoke, Greene knew he and his 40 employees were in for trouble.

Later, Colonel Greene issued the following statement:

> "After passing the jail and coming up the principal street, Mr. Dwight endeavored to stop one of the ringleaders, who was at the head carrying a red flag, and turned him back when one of the men shot at him, at a distance of only a few feet, evidently shooting over his head. I immediately shot, which was a signal to shoot, and the four leaders of the mob fell. The mob scattered in all directions. I immediately ordered all the boys to retire to my house and not shoot anymore under any circumstances, and for all to get together and keep together to avoid individual collision."

Colonel Greene sent a telegram to Izabál, the governor of Sonora, requesting help. "Urgent. Bring troops with you. Don't stop at Imuris. Take special train. Situation serious. About 40 killed. I will meet you at Naco with train to bring you here." Emilio Kosterlitzky's *rurales* (rural police) were based in Magdalena, a long distance from Cananea. It was estimated that it would take him two days with his forces to reach Cananea. They rode horseback at great speed without stopping, and in twenty-one hours reached Cananea, where Kosterlitzky imposed martial law.

Captain Tom Rynning of the Arizona Rangers temporarily resigned his position as commander of the Rangers and enlisted as the head of the Naco volunteer group that traveled by train to Cananea. When they crossed the border at Naco, the American volunteers were sworn into the Mexican Army – an historic event.

After the *rurales* rode into Cananea and the Naco volunteers arrived, there was little gunfire. With the proclamation of martial law, a deathly calm settled in. Word went out to all quarters: "All persons, Mexican and American, are to remain in their houses. Anybody found on foot in the streets after dark will be shot."

Colonel Greene issued his own orders as follows: "There must be no shooting for any cause tonight. All Americans will obey strictly the orders issued. We are going to have law and order in this camp and we are going to have it quick. There is no cause for alarm any longer. Go to your homes and go to bed. Myself, in company with Colonel Kosterlitzky and the governor, will be on patrol duty with the *rurales* for the remainder of the night."

On the following morning, 100 soldiers arrived and camped just outside of Cananea. The day thereafter, twice as many arrived, but by then, Kosterlitzky had everything well in hand.

General Torres, the commander of the Mexican Army unit, addressed the crowd on Sunday morning. "Anyone not back at work in two days will be drafted into the Army and sent to fight the Yaqui Indians."

The strike was over, but the repercussions went on. This event is believed to be the "spark that ignited the Mexican revolution."

In a letter written to his sister, Frances Holbrook, in Beloit, Kansas, dated July 28, 1906, Marion Williams wrote:

> "I supose you have heard of the Cananea trouble I was their their was about thirty five men killed in all Six or Seven americans and the balance mexicans it looked like was dilbaret I did not take any part in the trouble as I have every thing in this country and I could not aford to take part in the fight and now everything is quiet and no more trouble and I do not think their will be as there is five hundred Soldgers Stationed at Cananea to keep down trouble….
>
> (signed) your Brother, Marion Williams."

WALKING IS NOT ALL TAKEN UP – 1908

"Walking is not all taken up, Mr. Williams."

These words rang in Marion's ears as he stomped in anger out of the Nacozari Railroad Depot in October of 1908, where he shipped more than 1,000 head of cattle every November.

For many years, Marion had driven his herd from his Santa Rosa Ranch to the railroad spur at El Tajo, and it was necessary to arrange in advance for rail cars to be waiting at the holding pens and loading chutes there.

Frustrated by the indifference of the Nacozari depot manager, the lack of urgency in establishing a fixed date, and with the stinging words, "Walking is not all taken up, Mr. Williams," still buzzing in his head, Marion snapped.

"You are right. Therefore, I will walk my cattle from my ranch to the American border."

And he did just that...driving a massive herd the 70 miles from his Santa Rosa Ranch along the Nacozari railroad tracks to the holding pens in Agua Prieta, Sonora, Mexico. Being driven this great distance with little opportunity to graze or drink water along the way, the cattle lost weight. Upon arriving in Agua Prieta, they were put in "wet" pens, where they filled their bellies with water, and regained the lost weight, an important factor for two reasons:

Cattle were weighed by U.S. Customs to determine the amount of import duties to be imposed, as well as the amount of money to be paid by the buyer to the seller. Sale terms were agreed on by both parties prior to actual cattle delivery, which was usually made FOB (freight on board) at Douglas.

In 1909, a new manager at Nacozari was hired by the railroad, and a few months prior to the usual shipping date, he called upon Marion and said, "Mr. Williams, we have not heard from you about your shipping requirements for this year. Except for last year, we know you have always shipped with us, and we would like to continue that relationship. If you will tell us when and where you want the rail cars spotted for loading, we will be happy to provide your accommodation."

"Accommodation? I had a fine experience walking my cattle from my ranch to Douglas last fall, and I want you to know one thing for sure."

"What is that, Mr. Williams?"

"I intend to drive my cattle to Douglas again this fall, and remember, 'walking is not all taken up'."

PANCHO VILLA RIDES INTO OUR LIVES – 1914

The name Pancho Villa was well-known to the Williams family in the second decade of the twentieth century. His true name was Doroteo Arango Arambula. He took the name Villa which was the name of an old bandit chief. He was born in San Juan del Rio, Durango, on June 5, 1877.

It is believed that when he was 18, Villa's favorite sister, 16-year old Mariana, was raped by the son of the vicious *patrón*, Don Augustín Lopez Negrete. Villa took revenge, riddling the body of the unarmed youth with bullets before leaving home to join an outlaw band. Thus began the 22-year saga of Pancho Villa as he crossed three southwestern states and northern Mexico, as well as the path of the Williams family.

Pancho Villa's first encounter with our family took place early one Tuesday morning, on September 1, 1914. Ben Williams (Sr.) was washing his father, Marion's, new Franklin air-cooled touring car on the front lawn of their home on Seventh Street. Ben, 13, an eighth-grader, was surprised when the next-door neighbor, Francisco Elias, approached, asking, "Ben, do you know how to drive this car?"

Wealthy and influential, Mr. Elias owned a ranch in Sonora as well as the home on Seventh Street. He would become Governor of Sonora, then Secretary of Agriculture under Presidente Elias Calles from 1924 to 1928.

"Yes, Mr. Elias, I can drive this car."

"Good. I have to go to the depot to meet the Golden State Limited at 10, and my car won't start. Pancho Villa and his staff are coming from El Paso and are expecting me to drive them around town. Can you do it?"

"Of course."

They arrived just as the train pulled in, and Villa and nine of his *pistoleros* (body guards) climbed into and onto the car with Villa, Elias and Ben in the front seat. Three body guards rode in the back seat, and three on each running board, their weight causing the vehicle to ride on its axles.

Ben F. Williams, Sr., at age when he drove Pancho Villa in his father's Franklin air-cooled automobile

Ben chauffeured the group around Douglas, and then took them to the Douglas Chamber of Commerce luncheon honoring Villa, who had recently proclaimed himself governor of Chihuahua.

Ben's father, Marion, attended the luncheon, and reported that Villa didn't bother with silverware, eating with his fingers like an animal and spilling food on his clothing.

1912 Franklin Torpedo, air-cooled touring sedan, used by Ben F. Williams, Sr. to drive Pancho Villa

Marion owned and operated the Santa Rosa Ranch in Sonora. The ranch was well-stocked with more than 1,500 head of cattle. One day in 1915, one of Marion's cowboys came riding in to inform him that Pancho Villa had sent a military detachment to his ranch to "rustle" 300 head to take back to camp to feed Villa's troops, whereupon Marion saddled his horse and rode out to meet the detachment.

"You know those cattle are mine. If you take them, I will have no choice but to resist. Why don't you go to my neighbor's ranch? He's an American by the name of Sherman and he has left the country. Take his herd…and we won't have to fight."

Villa had fallen in and out of favor with various leaders of the Republic of Mexico between 1910 and 1915, as well as fighting Carranza for the presidency. He was friendly with our President Woodrow Wilson, until Wilson recognized Venustiano Carranza as the president of Mexico on October 2, 1915.

Infuriated, Villa gathered his forces and set out to destroy Carranza. His plan was to capture Agua Prieta across the border from Douglas, as well as the Mexican Customs House with its known cache of money from collected duties.

Villa brought his troops out of Chihuahua into Sonora, and after a perilous march through the mountains, assembled them south of Agua Prieta to fight Carranza's army.

In the meantime, our government permitted Carranza's forces to move by rail from Eagle Pass, Texas, to Douglas, where they crossed our border into Agua Prieta to reinforce their own garrison. Once there, they dug deep trenches, strung barbed wire, and borrowed high-powered electric lights from our military. The illumination of Agua Prieta blinded Villa's troops, thus making it possible for Carranza's army to successfully resist Villa's attacks.

The United States military had positioned artillery units in the foothills north-east of Douglas overlooking Agua Prieta. Their commanding officer sent word to the Mexicans, that if there was any fighting or shelling by Mexicans on American soil, his artillery – already in position – would decimate Agua Prieta in a barrage that would leave not one adobe brick on top of another.

Even so, artillery shells and rifle bullets found their way into and around Douglas where the residents, including youngsters, climbed atop railroad cars parked on the sidings at the depot and watched the battle.

"Rawhide Jimmy" Douglas owned the home at the corner of Tenth Street and D Avenue at the time. Mr. Douglas sold the house to Dad and moved to Montreal, Canada. In June, 1943, he wrote a letter to Dad saying that during the battle on October 29 and 30, 1915, a bullet had come through the roof and fallen on the bed in their master bedroom. He and Mrs. Douglas went downstairs for several hours until the battle subsided, and then went back to bed.

The Williams home is now a museum – the Douglas-Williams House Museum. This museum is now headquarters of the Douglas Historical Society, as well as the Cochise County Historical Society and the Douglas High School Alumni Association.

Douglas home through which a spent rifle bullet pierced the roof immediately to the right of the chimney onto the bed in the master bedroom during Pancho Villa's attack on Agua Prieta in 1915.
Arizona Historical Society/Tucson – Douglas, Arizona, Mayor Williams' Home

A rare picture of Pancho Villa, taken in Mexico City after his rebel forces had captured all of Mexico. *Arizona Historical Society/Tucson - Library/Archives. AHS# 48106.*

Generals Alvaro Obregon, Pancho Villa and John J. Pershing; immediately behind Pershing, to the right, is his aide-de-camp, 1st Lt. George Patton. *Photo courtesy of Arizona Historical Society, Tucson. AHS# 46445.*

Dad watched the two-day battle with friends from the roof of the Gadsden Hotel which he owned at one time with Ezra J. "Bud" Warner.

"We watched both sides firing at each other," Dad said. "At one point, Villa and his men decided to besiege the city with cannon fire. They strapped a small cannon on the back of a horse with the barrel aimed out over the horse's rear. Two men led the horse to the front lines, turned it around, loaded the cannon, and lit the fuse. There was a terrific explosion and the horse went flying heels over head. They didn't try that tactic again."

After several defeats, Villa and his troops headed back east to Chihuahua. On their way, they killed an American at Rancho Las Palomas out of pure hatred for *gringos*. The next day, March 9, 1916, at Columbus, New Mexico, 500 of his men attacked at 4:12 a.m. They caused great damage, burned buildings and killed 17 Americans, eight soldiers, and nine civilians, including one woman.

When Dad and his partners bought the Rancho Las Palomas Ranch in 1942, one of the assets was a home in Columbus, New Mexico, used as the American ranch headquarters. A great number of pockmarks in the plaster of the exterior walls from Villa's bullets were still in evidence in 1943 when I stayed in the house.

Following the Columbus event, President Woodrow Wilson ordered General John J. "Blackjack" Pershing, who was stationed at Fort Bliss, Texas, to assemble his troops and pursue Villa into Mexico. For eleven months, 10,000 troops under his command pursued the Villistas. Never once encountering Villa, Pershing and his troops were recalled to the U.S.

Villa continued his raids in northern Mexico until some of his friends secured a grant of amnesty from the Mexican government whereby he would have to agree to never fight the government again. Tired and aware that he could never climb to his former political and military heights, he accepted the terms.

Three years before his death at the age of 40, the Mexican government gave Pancho Villa the 24,000-acre Canutillo Ranch and unlimited funds for farm equipment, building materials and tools – and large pensions for his men.

The bandit – now country squire – built roads, farmed, and educated dozens of children. It seemed the murderous thug/Robin Hood had found peace at least.

Then on a small bridge in bright sunshine on Friday, July 20, 1923, Villa and three loyal bodyguards were executed. The seven heavily-armed assassins who ambushed Villa's Dodge touring car on the way to Parral were charged, tried and released for lack of evidence.

During the period of unrest caused by Pancho Villa, Camp Harry J. Jones was built, and staffed with 25,000 American soldiers. Until recently, trolley car tracks ran the length of Tenth Street from the camp into the center of Douglas, and on to the Mexican border.

When Daisy and I built our home in 1962, it was on the site of the old military camp. While digging the footings, we unearthed military brass buttons, buckles and one old whiskey bottle.

When I was a freshman at Douglas High School in 1944, I found an unexploded artillery shell on the side of Saddlegap Mountain east of Douglas. I placed it in the compartment on the back of my motor scooter and drove home, bouncing all the way. I mentioned my "find" during supper that evening; Dad wanted to see it immediately. I took him to the carriage house behind our home, and when he saw it, he called the Douglas police department, and they called Fort Huachuca, who sent a bomb squad to retrieve my deadly treasure.

I was indeed fortunate the shell didn't explode during its rough trip home in the compartment in the motor scooter. At the time, I was just two years younger than Doroteo Arango Arambula when he began his historic ride through southwestern history and into and out of our lives.

Letter from Jimmy "Rawhide" Douglas to Ben F. Williams, Sr.

Montreal June 29, 1943

Dear Ben:

I am so glad to have you in our house and am sure you and your family will like it.

James hopes some day to buy back his mother's piano for his boys after the war is over - so try and bear this in mind and don't sell it to anybody. It was my father-in-law's wedding present to my wife in Nov. 1891 and was delivered at the Senator Mine 12 miles south of Prescott where the Company had allowed me to build a board house that cost $1,200. It is a good piano of very good tone and sounds better than pianos now being made.

There is a hole in the ceiling in the bedroom made by one of Villa's bullets in his attack on Agua Prieta. We were in bed at the time, and moved downstairs for an hour or two.

I hope you found everything in good order and that Rose left things in good shape. You certainly got a bargain and I hope you will all be happy. Please remember me to your father and mother and to your wife.

Sincerely yours,

Douglas

WILD INDIANS ON THE WARPATH – 1915-1939

My cousin, Dell E. Williams, Jr., whom we called "Tooter," and I always looked forward to going to Granddad's ranch, the old John Slaughter place, 15 miles east of Douglas, Arizona. We spent the weekends with Granddad and loved to chase rabbits, quail and other wildlife. We chased rabbits across the fence along the international border to the neighbor's ranch in Mexico and sometimes were lucky enough to spot a coyote, javelina or some other worthy trophy, which we were never able to bag.

Our level of excitement would grow all during the week until we left early on Saturday morning to spend the weekend. Granddad was always very punctual. If he told us to be ready to go at eight o'clock on Saturday morning, we had better be there or he would leave without us.

One Saturday, we were five minutes late…just in time to see Granddad driving away. We hollered and waved. He saw us and waved back, but continued on his way. We were heartbroken. The next time we saw him, we said, "Granddad, we were there, you saw us, but you didn't stop."

"That's right, boys, but I told you to be there at eight o'clock, and if you were not on time, you'd miss the bus!"

On a cold weekend in January 1939, when Tooter was eight and I was ten, Granddad took us to the ranch. We were seated in front of a warm fireplace after supper. Granddad began telling stories about the olden days when he was ranching in Old Mexico southeast of Cananea, Sonora. Tooter and I sat spellbound, soaking up his tales and experiences. During a brief pause, Tooter asked, "Granddad, did you ever see any wild Indians on the warpath?"

Author holding dead rattlesnake, while Tooter looks on

"Well, about 24 years ago, in 1915, it was almost dusk at the Santa Rosa Ranch. Young Ben, your father, who was about your age," he said, pointing at me, "and I were washing dishes after supper. We were alone at the ranch, and as I dried a plate, I looked out the window across the yard toward the corrals, and noticed a feather come up beyond the fence. It quickly disappeared, but in a few moments, that feather popped up again. I became concerned because a band of Apache Indians had been reported marauding and killing in our area. When I saw that feather appear again over the corral fence, I whispered to young Ben, 'Walk slowly to the corner and get the 30-40 rifle. Young Ben did as he was told and brought the gun to me.

"It was getting darker outside, but I could still make out things in the twilight. It was a warm summer evening, so the window above the sink was open. I laid the rifle slowly and carefully on the windowsill and pointed it toward the fence. In a moment, the feather came up again, and I took dead aim, fired, and the feather disappeared!

"In a little while, I said to Ben, 'Let's slip quietly out to the corral and see if they've gone.'

"When we got to the corral and peeked over the fence, we were really surprised, for there on the ground lay a dead animal. Lo and behold! I'd killed the best damn mule I ever owned!

"That son-of-a-gun had been on the backside of the corral fence and, as a mule will sometimes do, he let his ears droop and then would occasionally raise one to flick away an insect. I surely thought that ear was an Indian's feather.

"And that, boys, was the only wild Indian I ever saw on the warpath."

Governor Raúl H. Castro

THE PROPHECY – 1924

One fine spring afternoon, Raúl H. Castro and Henry Zipf, law partners, and I were seated in my office telling stories, as lawyers are wont to do. We were all good friends and graduates of the University of Arizona School of Law.

We were having a grand time listening to Raúl tell of being born in Cananea, Sonora, Mexico, 60 miles southwest of Douglas. When he was a small child, Raúl's family moved to Pirtleville, four miles west of Douglas, where most of the Phelps Dodge smelter workers lived.

Raúl attended school in Douglas, and on the 4th of July, 1924, he and several of his eight-and-nine-year-old friends, all boys, gathered at the Tenth Street Park.

Although Governor George W.P. Hunt was running for re-election and delivering a campaign speech, the real reason the youngsters showed up was for the free refreshments: hot dogs, hamburgers and sodas. Raúl and his buddies didn't want to miss out on this great opportunity.

Governor Hunt, a heavy man, always wore a walrus moustache and a white linen suit, even on hot days. The press called him "The Old Walrus." He was not only Arizona's first governor after statehood, February 14, 1912, but was governor seven times, both territorial and state.

An eloquent speaker, Hunt extolled the virtues of the young state and the grand and glorious United States with opportunity abounding everywhere.

"Anybody can be whatever they want to be. It's just a matter of doing it…opportunity exists everywhere. Take for example that little Mexican boy right there," he said, pointing directly at Raúl. "Who knows? One day, that little Mexican boy could grow up to be governor of this fine state of Arizona."

Little did he know that Raúl Castro, through supreme determination and perseverance, would be elected Governor of Arizona in 1975. He was Arizona's first Hispanic governor, and only the third Hispanic governor in the United States.

Indeed, opportunities do exist, and prophecies do come true. In 1979, the Tenth Street Park in Douglas, Arizona, was renamed and dedicated "The Raúl H. Castro Park."

THE KNIGHTS AND THE BEES – 1936

In the summer of 1936, my cousin "Tooter" and I spent several weeks with our grandfather, Marion Williams, at his Willow Springs Ranch near Oracle Junction. It was a large cattle ranch – 90,000 acres – named for the springs and the abundance of desert willow trees there.

I was seven years old and Tooter was five, and the closest thing to a brother any boy could ever have or wish for.

One evening, Granddad said, "Boys, we're going to Tucson tomorrow to buy supplies for the ranch and a saddle for each of you."

Granddad didn't have to get us up the next morning; we'd been awake since daybreak planning exciting adventures with our very own new saddles. *Boy, oh boy! Life was good.*

The trip from the ranch to Tucson was time-consuming, as the rough dirt road was only occasionally bladed by a Pima County motor-grader. The winding road was narrow; encountering another vehicle was a rarity, but fun when it happened, as the drivers had to decide who would make room for the other first. The trip for two impatient youngsters seemed endless on this special day.

In 1936, there were only two air-conditioned buildings in Tucson: the Fox Theatre on Congress Street and the Pioneer Hotel on Stone Avenue, where Granddad "parked" us while he went shopping at Itule's Produce Market beside the railroad tracks.

After what seemed like forever, Granddad returned. "C'mon boys, let's go to Porter's Western Store up the street and look at the saddles."

Inside Porter's, at 808 N. Stone Avenue, we made our way through racks of fancy cowboy shirts, frontier suits, and colorful boots to the back of the store where Granddad's friend, Jack Egland, made fine saddles. There were wooden saddletrees in various stages being prepared for the special leather soon to be attached to their frames. The powerful aroma of strong glues and tanning extract, the greasy smell of Neat's-foot Oil, the sweet smell of Saddle Soap and the pungent scent of Mr. Egland's pipe tobacco made a long-lasting impression on us.

Finally, after much preliminary palaver with Granddad, Mr. Egland asked, "Marion, what can I do for you today?"

"Jack, I want new saddles for the boys."

"Fellers, I got just the ticket for you," he said, pointing to two brand new children's saddles. "Climb on and see how you like 'em."

"Benny, I like my saddle, but the stirrups are too long. How's yours?"

"Fine, Tooter, but my stirrups are too long too!"

Mr. Egland adjusted our stirrups as we sat in our new saddles on our imaginary steeds, grinning.

"The boys like the saddles; I like the saddles. We'll take 'em."

"Thank you, Granddad," we chorused gleefully. (You never saw two happier kids.)

Arriving back at the ranch just in time for lunch, the main meal of the day, we ate – but scarcely tasted – the meat, potatoes, string beans, *frijoles*, homegrown peach preserves and berry pie.

It was Granddad's custom to rest after lunch. On this particular day, he said, "After my nap, boys, we'll go for a ride."

Tooter and I pestered him until we talked him into going horseback riding before his nap. He asked his ranchhand, Damacio Valenzuela, to saddle the horses for us: Old Pinto, a gentle, ten-year-old mare for Tooter; and Chulo, a gentle, twelve-year-old bay gelding for me. We choked with pride and excitement seeing our own beautiful, handsomely-tooled, new-leather-smelling, Egland saddles on Old Pinto and Chulo, each bearing the "N Porter" emblem that graced some of the best saddles ever made.

Granddad saddled his gelding, Brownie, and we headed down a wide sand wash with a small stream of clear water running in it. We came to a place where green grass grew in the shade of an ancient cottonwood tree. Wanting to take his nap, Granddad said, "Boys, I'll rest here. You ride down the wash, but don't go too far…and don't get into any trouble."

He loosened the cinch on Brownie, took the bit out of his mouth and dropped the reins so he could graze on the lush grass. Then, taking off his hat, he stretched out in the shade to sleep.

We had ridden about an eighth-of-a-mile when we found ourselves between perpendicular banks 10 feet high. There, lo and behold, we discovered a hole about a foot in diameter in the bank at eye level. We could see bees coming and going out of the hole, as well as a honeycomb.

"Boy, oh boy, look at that Tooter! Let's find a lance and jab those critters. We can pretend we're knights with lances."

We found a yucca stalk about 12 feet long. By breaking off the top and stripping the branches, we made ourselves a fine lance. Tooter, being left-handed, took it in his left hand, and I grabbed it in my right hand. Although our wise old steeds were uncooperative, we managed to approach the bank, jab the lance into the hole and stir it up real good.

The bees came out, boiling mad, and took after us. Dropping our lance and spurring our steeds, we bolted away at a full gallop, hollering, "Granddad, Granddad, help! They're after us!"

Seeing the black cloud of infuriated insects, Granddad yelled, "Get away from me! Ride on up the wash and take those darn things with you."

Using his hat, he swatted the few bees attacking him, and we were galloping so fast, the swarm couldn't keep up, and finally gave up.

We waited awhile, then rode back to Granddad, who was even madder than the devil bees were. "I told you to stay out of trouble, and what have you done? You brought a swarm of bees up here to attack me!"

Chastened, we returned to the ranch house in silence, and helped put our mounts and saddles away.

We didn't dare tell Granddad that we were real knights or that we had deliberately thrust our lance into a beehive. We didn't dare tell Granddad that even knights with new saddles lose a joust now and then.

THE DEVIL'S WORK – 1936

My cousin Tooter and I spent the early part of the summer of 1936 at the Willow Springs Ranch, 30 miles northeast of Tucson, visiting Granddad and our grandmother, Nana. I was almost seven, Tooter was five, and the two of us were full of "Old Nick."

Dad had given me a Daisy Bull's-eye BB gun for Christmas, but I wasn't allowed to shoot it in town. Although Tooter and I knew how to shoot BB guns, my parents judiciously delayed the issuance of said air rifle until our summer visit. On our way to the ranch, we were both so excited we could hardly stand it, making the 160-mile trip from Douglas seem endless. With our young imaginations running wild, we spoke of shooting snakes, rabbits, coyotes, and perhaps a mountain lion. (The thought of shooting a chicken never entered our minds.)

As soon as we arrived, Tooter and I asked Granddad if we could take the BB gun and do some shooting.

"Be careful…and be sure to shoot it away from the house."

Nana, who with Granddad had lived on the ranch for two years, had a flock of fine brown laying hens in a chicken pen 70 yards from the ranch house. We meant to heed Granddad's admonition, but, locating no other game on our first foray into the hunting world, we found ourselves out by the chickens, where, without giving it a second thought, I shot at an old hen.

Hitting her somewhere in the feathers, she jumped at least two feet off the ground, squawking and fluttering her feathers as she ran away.

This seemed like great sport, so Tooter and I took turns shooting at a few more hens before losing interest and moving on to look for rabbits.

All too soon, we were called for supper. During the meal, Nana complained to Granddad, *"Viejo, una de mis gallinas tiene la pierna quebrada."* (One of my hens has a broken leg.)

Turning to us, Granddad asked, "Boys, have you been out shooting at the chickens?"

"Yes, Granddad, but all we did was make 'em squawk and jump in the air."

"Well," he said, "you broke the leg of one of your grandmother's favorite laying hens. She is very upset. We are going to have to kill that poor hen and have her for supper tomorrow night. When I go in to Tucson tomorrow, you will stay here at the ranch and help Nana pluck the feathers off that chicken."

Tooter and I had looked forward to going to Tucson with Granddad because he always bought us ice cream and "parked" us in the air-cooled lobby of the Pioneer Hotel, which, with the Fox Theatre, was the only other air-cooled business in Tucson in those days.

Crestfallen and angry, Tooter and I decided to get back at Granddad. In the barn, we found some old nails. Making sure no one was watching, we went out to the front of the house where Granddad parked his Chevrolet coupe in the shade. We knew he always drove his car forward when he was going anywhere, so, doing exactly as nine-year-old Bobby Denny taught me one day after school, we carefully propped a nail at an angle in front of each of the four tires.

The next morning, after making preparations to leave, Granddad said goodbye and went out to get into his car. Tooter and I ran to the front window and watched through the wooden blinds. Granddad started his engine, drove about 20 feet out into the hot sunshine and stopped. He turned off the engine and came back into the house for something he'd forgotten, and then left without noticing us hiding by the window. As he went to get back into the car, Granddad saw that the left front tire was flat. (In those days, punctured tires were not unusual.)

Opening the trunk, he took out the jack, the lug wrench and the spare, and changed the flat tire. It was late June, before the rains started, hotter than blazes at 110 to 115 degrees in the shade, and Granddad was now soaked with perspiration. Upon returning the tools to the trunk, Granddad noticed the left rear tire was flat, too.

Granddad looked as though he was ready to explode when along came Damacio Valenzuela, his ranch hand. "*Buenos dias, Don Mariano. Puedo ayudarle*?" (Good morning, Don Mariano. Can I help you?)

"*Si. Vamos a cambiar esta llanta*." (Yes. Let's change this tire.)

"*Muy bien, Don Mariano*."

Since the only spare was already in use, both men were sweating like stevedores from the oppressive heat by the time they patched the punctured inner tube, refilled it with the hand pump and remounted the second tire. Again replacing the tools in the trunk, Granddad checked the right front tire. Sure enough, it was hissing as it slowly lost its air.

By this time, Granddad and Damacio smelled a rat or two. (Tooter and I had been giggling for some time – careful however not to alert the overheated men to the fact that we were spying on them.)

"Three tires have gone flat. I'll bet there's a nail in that fourth tire, Damacio!"

Tooter couldn't stand it any longer. Sticking his head out of the open window, he yelled, "Yes, Granddad, there's a horseshoe nail in that one."

Granddad came tearing into the house, grabbed us by the scruffs of our necks, demanding, "What's gotten into you boys? First, you break your grandmother's chicken's leg with the BB gun, and now you've pulled this stunt. Tell me, what's gotten into you?"

"The devil made us do it, Granddad," said Tooter sheepishly.

"Well, we've got to do something about that," he said as he loosened and removed his belt. "I'll have to spank that devil right out of you boys."

"Z" brand owned by author; former owners Marion L. Williams and John H. Slaughter

THE SMOKIN Z – 1937

The letter "Z" is not only *The Mark of Zorro* glamorized by Hollywood's swashbucklers, but it is Arizona brand #00614 to be used on the right shoulder of cattle, horses, mules and asses in the Douglas, Cochise County, range.

John H. Slaughter moved to Arizona with his father-in-law, Amazon Howell, who used the "Z" on the left hip and jaw of cattle he brought into southern Arizona in 1879. Thereafter, Slaughter adopted the same "Z" brand, but placed his iron on the right shoulder instead, first registering his "Z" with the Arizona Livestock Sanitary Board on March 5, 1915, at San Bernardino, Arizona. It is one of the oldest, continuously registered brands in the county. Having been conveyed several times, the "Z" is now mine.

When Slaughter died in 1922, his widow, Viola, and family formed the "John H. Slaughter Ranch, Inc.," an Arizona corporation, which re-registered the brand on December 2, 1931.

When my grandfather, Marion L. Williams, purchased the ranch from Viola Slaughter in 1937, the brand was included in the sale. Granddad died on May 24, 1974, and I purchased the brand from his estate. I have leased the brand to various ranchers in southeastern Arizona; it is currently leased to the Johnson Historical Museum of the Southwest, where 15 head of Texas longhorns wear the "Z."

At one time, there were as many as 10,000 head of Mexican *corrientes* branded with the "Z." A *corriente* is a steer, or castrated male bovine, of mixed heritage and therefore of many colors.

A brand is a method of identifying livestock ownership. Unbranded cattle, or mavericks, may be subject to "appropriation" by a rustler who will mark them with his own brand, thus becoming the new, "rightful" owner.

A sure way of showing parentage is to separate horse colts and calves from their mothers with whom they have bonded. The offspring and their dams will make every attempt to reunite with each other.

To brand an animal, the end, or iron stamp brand, is heated over a campfire. When it reaches a high temperature, the iron is pressed against the hide of the animal for a few seconds, or long enough to burn off the hair and scar the skin so hair cannot grow back. The Egyptians permanently marked, or branded, their cattle as long as 3,000 years ago.

A properly-made stamp brand will have small notches at the points of the brand where the sides or lines come together. Since the heat is increased at these junctions, the notches are necessary to prevent hot spots which lead to open sores which will attract blowflies that lay eggs in these wounds. The blowfly larva, or screw worms, literally eat away the flesh of the animal, ultimately causing its death. Each new batch of larva hatches into more blowflies which in turn will lay more eggs, continuing the grotesque and deadly cycle.

A running iron brand is a curved branding iron used to "draw" on the animal's hide. Although the resulting brand is not as "legible" as a stamp iron brand and the difference between the two is fairly obvious, it was the branding iron of choice among thieves in the old west, who used it to copy legal brands.

Cattle cannot be transported more than a short distance without a certificate of inspection from an Arizona Livestock Inspector, who has visually inspected each animal's brand to make certain it corresponds to the legitimate registered owner.

One might consider a brand to be the same as the "proof of ownership" copyright symbol © used on literary and artistic works.

ARIZONA DEPARTMENT OF AGRICULTURE BRAND CERTIFICATE

NAME OF OWNER(S) WILLIAMS JR, BEN F

MAILING ADDRESS

NAME UNDER WHICH LIVESTOCK WILL BE SHIPPED OR SOLD

RANGE	LOCATION OF RANGE(S)	COUNTY
Douglas		Cochise

BRAND NUMBER 00614

Z

LOCATION OF BRAND

CATTLE RS
HORSE RS
SHEEP NO
GOATS NO

ANIMALS MUST BE BRANDED EXACTLY AS SPECIFIED

BRAND DESCRIPTION Z
EAR MARKS NO

I HEREBY CERTIFY THE BRAND AND MARKS APPEARING ABOVE WERE DULY RECORDED FOR THE OWNERS LISTED HEREIN AND THIS CERTIFICATE IS A FULL, TRUE, AND CORRECT COPY OF ENTRY AS THE SAME APPEARS ON THE RECORD IN THE OFFICE OF THE ARIZONA DEPARTMENT OF AGRICULTURE 1688. WEST ADAMS, PHOENIX, AZ 85007

AS WITNESS MY SIGNATURE AND THE DEPARTMENT SEAL HEREUNTO AFFIXED AT PHOENIX, AZ
THIS DATE Tuesday, April 25, 2006

STATE BRAND CLERK

ARIZONA DEPARTMENT OF AGRICULTURE

THIS CERTIFICATE WILL EXPIRE Sunday, May 15, 2011

Copy of most recent "Z" brand certificate from Arizona Department of Agriculture

The pond

THE POND – 1937-1987

What a joy the pond at the ranch house was – five acres in size, behind a stone-and-masonry dam, built long ago – prior to 1937, when I was eight and my cousin Tooter was five.

That was the year that our Granddad, Marion Williams, bought the San Bernardino Ranch from Viola Slaughter, John Slaughter's widow.

The house pond, fed by strong springs for thousands of years, was used by prehistoric Salado Indians as evidenced by the bedrock mortars ground into the volcanic malapais rock nearby.

Indian grinding mortars in Malpai adjacent to main springs

Artesian spring water flowing incessantly from the five-foot standpipe in the center of yet another pond was cool to the touch and sweet to the taste without brackish or mineral flavors. Exactly how a drink of water should taste!

Besides joy, the ponds sustained life for all manner of crops and creatures.

On the west side of the pond there was a henhouse in a fenced yard containing ducks and chickens that watered from the pond. Someone had to close the henhouse doors at night to keep predators from enjoying a midnight snack. Although plentiful, raccoons never bothered the poultry yard inhabitants, but fox, bobcats and coyotes were always alert for a succulent meal.

A valve on the east side of the dam permitted water to flow from the pond through a ten-inch pipe in the dam into the irrigation ditch running down to the fields below where alfalfa, barley and other crops grew. The finest watercress in all of southern Arizona grew in the everflowing ditches, and the orchard just below the dam provided delicious fruit.

Peaches – both freestone and clingstone – flourished, as did purple plums and sweet-as-candy greengage plums. Crab apples, apricots, pears and green apples did well. Grapes of the seed variety were prolific, providing great nourishment for the birds before we could harvest them.

Nana's peach and apple pies were wonderful treats following supper, and her apricot *empanadas* (turnovers) were sublime.

If water flowing to and past the orchard and the hay fields was not diverted, it continued on its path for half-a-mile to the Chinese farmers' fields below. Another large pond five miles below the ranch house at the Chinaman's Place provided water from two artesian springs – more than enough for irrigating an 80-acre field.

Yellow-bellied catfish as long as 10 inches grew in abundance in both ponds. It was great sport to cut a weeping willow limb, trim off the leaves and branches, and make a fishing pole. A line was attached to the pole with a bobber, a lead sinker and a hook. On the hook we placed angleworms dug up below the dam where they thrived in the soft, black soil. Never was a more enticing bait presented to a catfish. During grasshopper season in the summer, we used them for bait – not nearly as good as the angleworms.

Below and south of the dam, a hydraulic ram pumped water from another spring, which was located inside a covered three-foot-high concrete box, into an elevated 2,000-gallon steel tank mounted on a rock-and-cement foundation on a hill behind the ranch house.

Author, age 8, on left; cousin Tooter, age 6, on right; in kayak on pond made by author's uncle, Dell E. Williams, in early 1940s

Tooter, our other cousin Hector, and I learned to swim in the house pond, and the spillway was the private place where Tooter and I "enjoyed" our first smoke. High-grading one of Granddad's favorite Mexican cigars, we took it to the spillway. Our "enjoyment" didn't last long…we became violently ill and upchucked the fine lunch Nana served us at midday. Erroneously believing that boys could enjoy an after-lunch smoke like the grown men, we soon learned that cigars were for adults only, so we stuck to fishing.

On several occasions, we caught six or eight catfish, cleaned them and took them to the kitchen, where they were cooked for dinner. Nothing tasted better than those freshly-caught fish, but then catfish – in my estimation – is one of the best eating-fish anyway.

In the 1940s, my Uncle Morris and Aunt Ella Browder moved to the ranch. Aunt Ella was the collector of custom's secretary at the Douglas Port of Entry, traveling 15 miles to and from her job daily. Uncle Morris grew produce – corn, squash, cucumbers, watermelon and cantaloupe – which he sold to Bond Brothers Grocery in Douglas.

Uncle Morris ordered and "planted" two dozen pairs of jumbo frogs from Louisiana in the pond at the Chinaman's Place, where they flourished. They can now be found in most of the waters on the American and Mexican sides of the International border. Considered a delicacy, people often came from Douglas to gig, or spear, the jumbos for their legs.

Nana and a couple of workers built a shrine and a fishpond in the front yard of the ranch house. Using her collection of colored, pea-sized pebbles – which they embedded in the concrete – they spelled out the date of construction: September, 1942.

A constant spray of water from the center of Nana's pond provided oxygen for the goldfish she'd purchased at Newberry's store in Douglas. In 1945, the goldfish were transferred to the house pond east of the ranch house while their habitat was cleaned and repaired.

Years later, when Granddad drained the house pond to clean out accumulated silt, the entire bottom was covered with the most beautiful golden color you ever saw. The fish had multiplied and grown to ten to fourteen inches in length, and until I saw all the dead "goldfish," I never knew the fish lying on the bottom of the pond were carp.

The two other occasions the house pond was emptied was when there were some hellaciously heavy rains causing tumultuous floods the dam could not hold. When the spillway washed out, the new one was built at the northeast end of the dam and has since handled every flood.

When I returned to Douglas to practice law in 1956, several friends and I decided to entice ducks to the house pond. Gordon Brown, the undertaker; Dr. Robert E. Montgomery, the physician; Paul Whalen, owner of Paul's Jewelers; and I ordered duck food from the eastern United States comprised of water plants –water lilies, hyacinths and cattails–which we planted in the pond. Before long, there was luxurious growth the wild ducks found irresistible, while we, the hunters, found the waterfowl delicious.

Shelley Richey, a Douglas lawyer, and I netted crappie and eight-inch bass in the dam near Nacozari, Sonora. We transported them to the ranch in an old ice chest, stopping every few miles along the way to give the fish a good shot of oxygen from a compressed oxygen bottle. They flourished.

Walter Lawson, Senior Vice President and Western General Manager of Phelps Dodge Corporation at Douglas, enjoyed fishing with us. On one occasion he had the tin shop at the PD smelter make a container in which he placed bass caught at Angostura Dam south of Douglas. He then had a pilot fly him and the bass back to Douglas where he put the fish in the bathtub at his home overnight. The next day, Shelley Richey and I took the bass out to the ranch and released them in the pond.

Not long after that, George Stephens, Sr., a neighboring rancher, decided to drain his pond to deepen it. When young George Stephens ("Cowboy" to us) notified me, I took several buckets to the Stephens' pond where, as it was being emptied, I caught two-inch blue gill by the hundreds as they sailed out of the drainage pipe. I put them in the house pond where they joined their cousins, the native catfish, bass and crappie.

What with the ducks, the fish, the jumbo frogs and an occasional goose, we had our own private game preserve and enjoyed it to the fullest extent until Granddad put a pigpen next to the water at the northern end of the pond. Not only did it stink, but the water was polluted and the catfish developed parasites in the flesh on their sides. We could no longer eat them.

The ranch headquarters and ponds were sold eventually to the Johnson Historical Museum of the Southwest, who, along with the U. S. Department of the Interior, Fish and Wildlife Service, preserve the ranch.

The Fish and Wildlife Service poisoned all the now-predator jumbo frogs and the exotic fish and have, in 1987, restocked the ponds with native, endangered species: the Yaqui chub, Yaqui top minnow and Yaqui catfish.

Our own private game preserve is gone, but the ponds live on.

WILL IT HOLD? – 1938-1939

In 1938 and 1939, the Mexican government built a dam 70 miles south of Douglas, Arizona, in the state of Sonora on the Bavispe River. The dam was called Angostura, meaning narrow, and was built of reinforced concrete between two high canyon walls of solid rock, known to the inhabitants as *las angosturas*.

The chief American engineer on the dam and his ten-year-old son, Bobby Black, were next-door neighbors living in Douglas for the two years it took to complete the dam. Being the same age, Bobby and I became good friends.

As the lake behind the dam filled, the rising waters inundated thousands of acres of fertile farmland along the Bavispe River, including, it is said, the farms of numerous Chinese opium poppy growers. As it neared completion, the concerns of those living and farming below the dam grew in direct proportion to the increasing volume of stored water in Angostura Lake, which eventually reached 18 miles in length and 3 miles at its widest point.

In desperation and great fear, the residents gathered to form a committee of seven men to investigate and inspect the dam itself for strength and stability. Choosing a leader, the delegation of seven set out at an appointed time, riding horseback up to the dam site. Upon arriving, they contacted the chief Mexican engineer, José Luis Anchondo. (His daughter would become a U.N. interpreter.)

"We have come to see if the dam is built correctly. We must determine its strength and sturdiness. We are the official inspectors selected by the people living south of the structure."

José Luis Anchondo graciously accompanied the mounted group, and on arriving at the base of the dam, announced with pride, "Here it is. Isn't she a beauty?"

"*Si*, it is pretty enough," said the appointed leader. "But will it hold?"

"Oh, *si*, it will hold," replied Señor Anchondo.

Whereupon, Juan Flores, the leader of the delegation, dismounted from his horse and approached the base of the massive concrete structure. After studying its towering height for a few moments, he kicked the base of *La Presa* (the dam) *de Angostura* with his hand-tooled leather boot.

Shaking his head, he returned to his horse, mounted with dexterity, and announced with superb officiousness, "It's safe. It will hold."

And with that, the members of the "posse" returned to their respective pueblos and farms to proclaim to one and all, "The dam is safe. It will hold."

Which it did, and still does 68 years later.

Large-mouth bass catch from Angostura Lake in 1958. From left: George A. Swanson, Western Comptroller, Phelps Dodge Corporation; author; Dr. Robert E. Montgomery, physician and surgeon from Douglas; Frank E. Fair, owner of Fair's Sports Shop, Douglas

MAKING HAY – 1939

In 1937, Granddad bought the San Bernardino Ranch from the John Slaughter Ranch Corporation. It had been owned by John Slaughter, the famous Sheriff of Cochise County, and was located in the extreme southeast corner of Arizona. Originally, the greater part of the spread lay in Mexico, and had been sold to Lieutenant Ignacio Peréz as the San Bernardino Spanish Land Grant in May of 1822.

In the early years of the 19th century, Lieutenant Ignacio Pérez, a 29-year-old career officer and a member of one of the most prominent land-holding families in Sonora, made application for permission to purchase the land grant. A native of Arispe, Sonora, Lieutenant Pérez's father, Don José Pérez Ortiz, owned the rich mines at Cananea. In 1821, the Republic of Mexico was successful in gaining its independence from Spain. A public auction was conducted early in 1822, and Pérez was permitted to purchase four *sitios*, approximately four square leagues, plus additional "overplus" or excess lands as then permitted under law. The total size was almost 100,000 acres, and his bid of 90 pesos plus fees was the winning bid.

When Granddad bought the place in 1937, the largest part of the ranch in Mexico had already been disposed of, leaving a cattle ranch in Arizona of 13,900 acres. It was good rangeland with several hundred acres of farmland. Slaughter drilled nine artesian wells. These supplemented the eight natural springs used by peaceful prehistoric people, the Salado Indians. On the mesa above the springs, they ground hollows in the solid volcanic rock to use as mortars for grinding seeds, natural grasses and beans, especially those from the abundant mesquite trees nearby. The resulting meal, or flour, was made into bread and cake.

A number of horses were needed for ranch work, such as riding fence, tending cattle and packing salt, supplies and fence materials. Granddad felt his horses were mistreated if they were not fed grain, so he grew barley in three large fields near the springs. The crop was of fine quality, providing a nutritious grain with large heads, and hay. A flake or two mixed with alfalfa made a good daily ration for Granddad's horses; they thrived on that diet.

The soil was rich, almost black; it would grow anything. Nana, my grandmother, grew cantaloupe, cucumber, watermelon, corn, squash, tomatoes, radishes, carrots, onions and various herbs. There was an orchard with apples, pears, greengage plums, quince and small clingstone peaches which she canned. Her green clingstones, preserved with cloves and other spices, were absolutely delicious…and my favorites.

Two Mexicans worked and lived on the ranch. One was married with a wife and three children; the other, single. When work required it, others were put on the payroll.

In June of 1939 – two months before my 10th birthday – I spent the summer at the ranch with Granddad and Nana. One morning at breakfast, Granddad said, "Tomorrow I am going to put you to work on the hay baling crew. We're going to bale barley in the big field down by the warm-water well."

"Great," I said. "Does the job pay?"

"Of course," he said. "A good day's work always deserves a good day's pay."

"What will my job be?" I asked.

"You are going to drive Old Bill."

"But, Granddad," I exclaimed with a look of disappointment on my face and an air of disapproval in my voice, "that's no job. All I'd do is follow that old nag around in circles all day long."

"Sit down and let me tell you something," he said. "In most of the things we do in life, there is one thing that is more important than all the others. In baling hay, the most important part is the energy it takes to compress the bales in the machine so they can be bound with wires to hold them together. In the case of hay baling, that energy is provided by Old Bill, who walks around in circles all day. In each circle, he makes the machine press the hay so that the wires can each be tied. There are three wires on each bale. A piston-like device pushes the hay, which is fed into the hopper, compressing it into a rectangular form and then releasing the pressure."

"Now, that horse won't move on his own," said Granddad. "Somebody has to make him walk to energize the baler. Your job is to make that horse walk around until all the hay is baled. So, you see, your job is the most important one of all."

"Why, sure, Granddad, I see now! Unless Old Bill is made to walk around, the hay is not baled."

"Exactly," said Granddad.

During hay baling season, the baler was set up in a corner of the field. It would usually take two to three days to bale a whole field. Our work day started at 4:30 a.m., when we ate a hearty breakfast of oatmeal, bacon, eggs, toast and coffee.

I had come of age – almost 10 years old – getting up at 4:30 in the morning with the men, having a large breakfast, then riding down to the field in the back of the big truck My job ran the whole show! I drove that horse in a circle all day long, from six in the morning until five in the afternoon. The horse pulled a singletree harness attached to a pole that compressed the hay once it had been put into the hopper. If the horse didn't work, the baler didn't run. It was a one-horse baler – slow, but effective.

We worked all day long, the salty perspiration rolling off our smelly bodies. And whether we were baling fine-leaved alfalfa or prickly-whiskered barley, the dust and chaff penetrating our clothing and inside our collars made us dirty, itchy and looking forward to our evening visit to the warm-water well 100 yards from the field.

Drilled by Slaughter in the early 1900s, this well was 10" in diameter with a 6'6" standpipe from which warm water flowed continuously, as artesian wells do. An unattractive covered tin springhouse gave us privacy for our baths.

What a wonderful memory, and a truly delightful experience: the ripping off of one's field-nasty clothes, lathering up with Lifebuoy soap, and rinsing off in the warm, pure liquid bubbling up from deep within the earth.

After a good supper in the ranch house, one of the men would bring out his guitar, and we would sing in surprising harmony. I learned to play the guitar, and to sing many of the Mexican songs popular at the time.

On reflection, life was good.

Was I paid? You bet I was…one dollar a day…and I was living high-on-the-hog.

THE JEEP – 1939

In 1939, Willys-Overland and Ford Motor Company each submitted plans and prototypes for a new four-wheel, light-reconnaissance vehicle to the United States Army.

Designed to replace old motorcycles and Ford Model T trucks, Willys' plans won the competition. The Ford model was called the "GP" (general purpose), which stood for "government 80-inch wheelbase reconnaissance car." Slurred, GP sounded like "Jeep," which stuck, although the vehicle was built according to Willys' plans for its "MB" model.

More than 350,000 Jeeps were built, and at the end of the war, a new one rolled off the assembly line every 90 seconds. A valuable vehicle during the war, the Jeep proved to be equally successful for civilian use, particularly for ranchers and outdoorsmen.

Dad purchased the first civilian model in Cochise County for use on his 286,000-acre Las Palmas Ranch in Mexico. When a four-wheel-drive vehicle was needed to cover the country, the Jeep was the only one available.

When our Jeep was new, Dad brought it to town and let me drive it. I was 16 and thought I knew everything. Driving around Douglas one night, I was playing "ditch" with a friend who was chasing me in his car; the object of "ditch" being to "get away" or lose one's pursuer. Not realizing the pursuer in this case was Wirt French, a Douglas police officer, I ditched him and went home. I learned from my father the next day that I had "ditched" a long-time policeman with a tough reputation. In a community of 13,000 people, everybody knew everybody else's business, and I was driving the only civilian Jeep in town. I caught the dickens from Dad and was grounded for two weeks – for what I considered to be a long spell.

Headquarters of Las Palmas Ranch showing Jeep and Ben, Sr.'s Chevrolet (custom built to include oversized wheels, tires and springs, radiator and gas tank, steel skid plate under transmission).

Although he never learned to pilot an aircraft, Dad bought a Beechcraft Bonanza airplane so he could be flown back and forth from Douglas to the ranch. There was no airstrip at the ranch, so a flat pasture miles from headquarters was used, although it was covered with dangerous gopher holes, prairie dog mounds and tree stumps. As a better landing strip was needed, I volunteered to build it. After consulting with Larry Campbell, Dad's pilot, we laid it out.

Originally, horses or mules pulled the fresnos, although mules were preferred because they were stronger, but the Jeep in compound low and four-wheel-drive had amazing pulling capacity. Using it to pull the fresno, a metal dirt scoop with two handles, one of the cowboys and I cleared the strip. I drove, while a man on foot held onto the handles. When the scoop was full of the dirt scraped off the prairie dog mounds, he raised the handles, spreading the dirt like a land plane. A third man chopped and cleared mesquite trees, shrubs and yuccas and Dad's airstrip was finished.

In addition to using the Jeep to clear the airstrip, Benjamín Sandoval, my sidekick, and I used it to haul salt blocks to the widespread cattle waters. At one time, 11,000-head of Mexican crossbred steers roamed the ranch, and we had to make sure they had water. When there wasn't enough wind to turn the windmills, we used gasoline pump jacks to pump water from the wells.

If a gasoline engine used to power a pump jack quit working, we would jack one wheel of the Jeep up off the ground, and use the spinning, elevated wheel to turn the pump jack belt and flywheel.

The Jeep was kept so busy during dry seasons that it never cooled off. It was an amazing vehicle and so versatile it would go anywhere and could almost climb trees. It was my private vehicle for the summer I worked at the ranch, and even though I drove it over 100 miles back and forth to the ranch from Douglas many times, it never gave me any problems.

While I was away at New Mexico Military Institute, Dad lost the Las Palmas Ranch when the Mexican government expropriated it. I never saw the Jeep again.

Nogales headquarters of Rancho Las Palomas in 1940s; Victor Gabilondo's quarters on the left.

RANCHO LAS PALOMAS – 1942

Around the turn of the 20th century – using gold coins – two Americans, Wood and Hagenbarth, purchased 13 contiguous, privately-owned, titled and deeded ranches located along the New Mexico border in the state of Chihuahua, Mexico, thus forming the 2,270,000-acre Palomas Land and Cattle Company, the largest ranch in North America. The 3,547-square mile ranch extended from a point 14 kilometers west of Juarez, Chihuahua, 168 miles along the U.S. border to the Chihuahua-Sonora state line.

The ranch was almost the combined size of Rhode Island's 1,231 square miles and Delaware's 2,396 square miles; and more than four times the 825 square miles of the famous King Ranch in south Texas.

Bill Greene, son of Colonel William Cornell Greene, the developer of the enormous Cananea copper mines, learned that the Palomas Ranch was for sale. The Security First National Bank of Los Angeles was asking $1 million for the property it had acquired through a mortgage foreclosure.

Bill Greene brought the property to the attention of four experienced cattlemen: Ben F. Williams, Sr. of Douglas; Alfonso Morales of Douglas and Agua Prieta; Al Kalin, wealthy livestock feeder and owner of the San Pasqual Land and Cattle Company, Brawley, California; and Bill's stepfather, Charles Wiswall of Cananea. Colonel Greene, Bill's father, also owned the Baca Float Ranch near Prescott, as well as ranches near Cananea and in the San Rafael Valley of Santa

Cruz County, Arizona.

On February 21, 1942, the five partners purchased the ranch, paying $500,000 for the land and $500,000 for the 16,543 head of cattle, many wearing the "W" brand on the jaw and the "H" on the shoulder, reflecting the names of the original owners, Wood and Hagenbarth.

In addition to the headquarters, Hacienda de los Nogales, the inventory included all ranch equipment, 75 mules, 75 horses, a 10-gauge shotgun and a Browning automatic rifle, or BAR, used in World War II. This gas-operated, air-cooled portable rifle was capable of firing 200 to 350 rounds a minute and was illegal for civilian use; however, the ranch security guard, Orozco, used it to protect livestock from rustlers.

The purchase agreement provided that land lying east of the east fence line in the Los Moscos pasture could be sold for not less than 25 cents an acre, and the land lying west of that fence line could be sold for not less than 50 cents an acre; providing however, that proceeds from such sales were to be applied to reduce the purchase price.

When Dad and his partners were inspecting the ranch prior to purchase, he noticed an abundance of bleached bovine bones around the alkaline, brackish waters of the vast east pasture, Los Moscos. He felt that there were far fewer cattle than the bank claimed, and proposed that the $500,000 allocated for the cattle be divided by 16,543 to determine the value of each head, which turned out to be $31.

He proposed that the buyers pay the bank an additional $31 per head for any cattle over and above 16,543, and the buyers receive a $31 credit for the actual number of cattle under 16,543. The cattle were rounded up per the contract, which recited:

> "First parties agree to promptly cause the cattle located on the lands of Cia. Palomas in Mexico be rounded up so that an accurate count of all cattle on hand may be had. It is agreed (1) that representatives of both parties shall meet in Hachita, New Mexico, on the morning of February 28, 1941, (2) that the wagons shall start on the morning of March 1, 1941, and (3) that such count shall be effective in the most practical manner agreeable to both parties, taking into

> consideration weather conditions, range conditions, etc. Each animal counted shall be marked by clipping its tail, and all unbranded animals of weaning age shall be, at such time, branded. No 1941 calf shall be counted. At the time of taking the count mentioned, old cows, which are to be selected by second parties, and coming yearling steers, shall be gathered and held in a pasture agreed upon by both parties, for the purpose hereinafter mentioned."

As Dad suspected, the actual number of cattle turned out to be fewer by 1,000 head, and the buyers received $31,000 credit on the purchase price.

As required by the contract, the new partners restocked the ranch to increase the size of its cattle herds to a minimum of 25,000, and purchased 306 young registered Hereford bulls to improve the calf crop, as most of the many ranch bulls were old and "spent."

The inventory roundup began in Hachita, New Mexico, on March 1, 1941. Ordinarily, six fence camps were in operation with four to six hands in each camp. During the roundup, however, extra cowboys were hired with 25 assigned to each chuckwagon. The ranch owned three chuckwagons in all, but only two were used for this roundup, each bossed by a *caporal*, or wagon boss. Each crew was responsible for its own herd as it worked one portion of a pasture, while the other crew worked another part of the same pasture.

"Chapo," a chuckwagon swamper, in front of a chuckwagon

Each chuckwagon had its own cook and one swamper, who peeled potatoes, hauled firewood, built fires, washed dishes, made coffee, and performed any other duties or chores requested by the cook, including "jerking" beef. To prevent blowflies from laying eggs that became flesh-eating maggots on leftover beef, the swamper sliced, salted and hung the thin strips of meat on wires overnight.

Dutch ovens and frying pans were used to

cook; beans were boiled in large enamel pots; and the "always available" coffee was boiled in three-gallon, blue-speckled enamel coffeepots.

My favorites were the "cookies," the hot biscuits made in the Dutch ovens, topped with boiled syrup made from the hard, brown sugar cones, *piloncillos*.

Chuckwagon. *Photo courtesy of Arizona Historical Society, Tucson. AHS# BN23094.*

If possible, the wagons camped where potable water was available; but if such campsites could not be found, the large drums of water carried on each wagon were used.

Cattle were driven 10 to 12 miles a day, and at times, were driven at night in order to reach water where they could rest and drink. When rounded up, the herds of cattle were dehorned, vaccinated, earmarked, branded, and doctored with Smear 62 if they had wounds full of maggots. The cattle to be counted were marked by clipping their tails, and the bull calves were castrated.

Cowpunchers were paid the equivalent of $30 a month plus grub. They were paid in pesos. Wagon bosses were paid $75 a month plus grub. Windmill crews usually delivered provisions to the fence-building crews; however, on occasion, the crews would ride in to headquarters and take provisions back to camp on pack horses and pack mules.

The headquarters, Hacienda de los Nogales, was located at the base of the

Sierra Madre mountains in northern Chihuahua, 15 miles south of Antelope Wells, New Mexico, the U.S. port of entry. When cattle were shipped into the states, they crossed at Antelope Wells or Columbus, New Mexico; or at Lamentos, or Berendo, Chihuahua, the Mexican ports of entry.

Several rooms in the west wing of the Hacienda de Los Nogales were occupied by six to eight hands – some with families, some single. A couple of the rooms were reserved for travelers who arrived on foot, by horseback, muleback or in wagons. They were welcome to stay rent-free for a week or two, and could eat free of charge in the cowboys' dining room.

Each room in the headquarters had a fireplace, as the elevation was 5,000 feet, making it cold in wintertime. Although a Kohler plant provided electricity for lights at night, all cooking was done on wood stoves. If the plant was ever running in the daytime, a maid was ironing.

Ranch supplies such as beans, lard, flour and coffee beans were purchased in bulk at Casas Grandes, Chihuahua, two hours away by truck over a rough dirt road. Five or six tons of beans, half-a-ton of sugar, and half-a-ton of green coffee beans were bought at one time, and were used to feed all the ranch hands and their families for six months.

While foods were rationed in the United States during World War II, there was always plenty of flour, sugar, beans, coffee, and *piloncillos*, as the natives, or "Chihuahuences," called the hard brown sugar cones which were bought by the case, many cases at a time. The white Mexican sugar came from cane, and was coarser and darker than American sugar, and much sweeter.

As the ranch purchase contract required that approximately 1,000 miles of fence be rebuilt and maintained, spools of barbed wire were purchased in rail-car-lots. Block salt for the cattle was also purchased by the carload and stored in ranch *bodegas* (warehouses) at Palomas, Chihuahua, and in the Hacienda de los Nogales to be distributed as needed.

The first summer I spent on the ranch was with Victor Gabilondo, the ranch superintendent, a childhood friend of Dad's. I have special memories of Victor and me trying to meet a chuckwagon at midday whenever possible, to partake of the good food and in particular, the hot Dutch oven "cookies" we sopped up with piloncillo syrup.

The next year, Victor married a lady from Bisbee and brought her to the ranch. Mary was a sweetheart; when she was around, the meals were always better and the quarters always cleaner. Victor and Mary's daughter, Cookie, lives in Hermosillo, Sonora, and their son, Victor, lived in Nogales, Arizona, where he was the Director of Public Works for Santa Cruz County before dying of cancer.

Another significant person I knew at the ranch was Charlie Johnson, the Mexican officer in charge of the port of entry at Berendo, Chihuahua, three-quarters of a mile west of Antelope Wells, the American port of entry. Charlie, a friendly man, spoke no English, which I found confusing as he had an Anglo name.

Charlie was good at stalking deer and killing them with his 22 rifle. He shared the venison with his friends, and was grateful whenever I could give him a box of 22 long-rifle ammunition, a rare commodity because World War II was going full blast and ammunition of all calibers was hard to come by.

While the Mexican port where Charlie Johnson lived was only a couple of adobe huts, the American port was nothing more than a small ranch house where the U.S. Customs officers, Mr. and Mrs. White, lived. Whenever Mr. White was away on business, Mrs. White handled the port alone.

Although the time I spent at Rancho Las Palomas was short, the memories I have shared with you will last a lifetime, as will those of my fine, sure-footed mare named *Cola Chueca*, or "crooked tail" because of the injury caused by coyotes when she was born.

I will treasure forever the sounds of cattle lowing, calves bawling, horses whinnying, coyotes howling, cowboys whistling and "yipping" as they drove the herds from place to place; and the strumming of guitars and Mexican songs in the evenings.

I can still smell the wood burning in the old cookstoves and campfires; the acrid smoke from burning hair as red-hot branding irons left their marks; the fresh scent of rain, the rich smell of strong coffee.

I can still taste trail dust, salted jerky, and the sweet piloncillo syrup on the hot Dutch oven "cookies."

What more could a teenaged boy then, or an old gentleman-cowboy now, ask for?

TRES PAPALOTES (THREE WINDMILLS) – 1943

I spent the summer of 1943 at the Palomas Ranch in Chihuahua, Mexico. Dad, one of the owners, and his partner, and his partner's friend, Red, came to spend a couple of days to look things over (actually to inspect the cattle and check range conditions). It had been a fine year with lots of rain and feed. The cattle were putting on weight and looked great.

The five of us got into the car and drove from headquarters, Hacienda Los Nogales, west to the Punto de la Sierra pasture. This was, as the name implies, the point of the mountain, on the northern end of the Sierra Madre mountain range.

The ranch was enormous – 2,270,000 acres, or 3,546 square miles – three times the size of Rhode Island and more than four times the size of the famous King Ranch in Texas.

It took about 40 minutes to drive to *Tres Papalotes* where there was a cattle water consisting of a large holding tank, two troughs and a windmill. We all got out, walked around the watering place and checked to see if the troughs were full. A slight breeze was blowing, and the windmill was pumping a good stream of water into the steel tank. There were cement bases and wells for three windmills, but only one mill was in place. Two had been removed.

The partner's friend, Red, said, "Ben, I noticed that there are foundations for three windmills here, but only one is installed. Why is that?"

Dad quickly responded, "Well, the reason for that is there's not enough wind for three windmills."

He said, "Oh, I see," and said nothing further.

The next morning when we were all gathered at breakfast, Red said, "You know, Ben, I've been thinking about that situation yesterday when you said there wasn't enough wind for three windmills, and I now understand it. I thought about it most of last night."

He proceeded to explain how one windmill would take the wind from the other two and thereby deprive the other two mills of the wind.

Everybody howled with laughter.

Now, folks, what do *you* think?

QUAIL ON TOAST – 1943

John Darling was a master mechanic and craftsman, as well as a U.S. immigration officer stationed at the Douglas port of entry.

In 1943, Darling designed and built a motor scooter powered by a 3/4-horsepower Cushman gasoline engine to which was attached a pulley on its flywheel. A simple clutch moved a platform back and forth creating tension on a V-belt, which then turned the rear wheel drive, propelling the scooter.

Two persons could ride on the wooden bench seat on top of the storage compartment built over the motor mounted on the platform. The scooter's top speed was 15 mph.

Dad bought the scooter for me when my pal, Al Brady, and I were freshmen at Douglas High School in 1944. When my grandparents, Marion and Nana, were staying in town for the weekend, Brady and I would go out to their San Bernardino Ranch to hunt and mess around.

After school on Friday, we would buy groceries, then pack the "grub," sleeping bags and toilet articles in the storage compartment in the scooter. My Winchester 22 rifle was a necessary part of our equipment.

Although it was only 13 miles from the Douglas International Airport to the ranch, it took us at least an hour on the scooter because of the deep corduroy condition of the road.

At the ranch house, we put our bedrolls and gear in the back bedroom because it had a fireplace where we would build a fire. While the room was warming up, we'd build another fire in the wood cook stove in the kitchen and fry hamburgers for supper.

As there was no television, and we weren't interested in the radio, Brady and I would sit in the warm bedroom telling stories.

One evening while cleaning and oiling my 22 rifle for the hunt the next morning, I accidentally pulled the trigger. To this day, only Brady and I know how that neat hole in the baseboard got there.

Whoever got up first in the morning started the fire in the stove and put on a pot of coffee. Dressed, we'd go out behind the barn 100 yards from the house and shoot three or four quail from one of the resident coveys. We cleaned them, rolled them in flour, salt and pepper, and cooked them in bacon grease until golden brown, and toasted white bread on the hot griddle. Quail on toast – no finer vittles could be found.

After our gourmet breakfast, we headed for the mesa across the pond from the house to search for Indian artifacts, old calvary uniform buttons, and saddle and harness buckles.

In 1822, when Spain sold the San Bernardino Land Grant to Lieutenant Ignacio Peréz, the mesa was called *La Mesa de la Avanzada* (Mesa of the Advance Guard). It provided a commanding view of the San Bernardino Valley in Mexico. Rock outlines of the streets where calvary had established a camp in July, 1885, can be seen today. Still in evidence are stone breastworks built to fortify the camp where Troop K of the 4th Cavalry from Fort Huachuca was stationed to protect John Slaughter and settlers from Geronimo, raiding renegade Apaches, and in 1915, Pancho Villa's men.

There are ruins of two old rock and mortar buildings: a commissary and officers' quarters with a large fireplace built in one corner. Even today, there are rumors of John Slaughter having buried treasures around the ranch. Years ago, my grandmother Nana, convinced the treasure was buried in one of the old stone houses, took a couple of workmen, and dug around the fireplace and in the four corners of each building, finding nothing.

There are remains of a stone fence where a horse corral once stood.

Besides collecting relics on the mesa, Brady and I often wandered across the border to Calderón Ranch through the five strands of barbed wire loosely strung between cedar and mesquite posts. The lakes at Calderón's were fed by artesian springs and provided a fine location for shooting a duck or two. Then we'd head back across the border to scout for rabbits, coyotes and bobcats.

After enjoying a delicious breakfast of quail on toast again Sunday, we continued our hunting and relic collecting until mid-afternoon. Then, packing our gear and bedrolls, Brady and I climbed on the scooter and, with great reluctance, headed back to town...two high school freshmen loaded with wonderful memories.

MODERN CONVENIENCES – 1944

How well I remember the summer of 1944! The Second World War was going on when my cousin, Tooter, and I spent the summer with our Aunt Ella and Uncle Morris Browder at the San Bernardino Ranch.

Although it was almost impossible to buy appliances in those days, they purchased a brand-new, modern Kelvinator, a kerosene refrigerator. It never got close to being cold enough inside to make ice cream, but Tooter and I were thrilled. Not only could we have ice in our lemonade on hot days, but we could make popsicles by freezing Koolaid. And, we could use the ice with salt for making ice cream in the hand-cranked mixer.

What a far cry it was from the past when we cooled water in an earthen *olla* hanging on the porch. A clay pot with a small neck, it was wrapped in burlap with a tin dipper hanging on its side. The rule was, if one took a drink, one had to fill the dipper with water and pour it all over the burlap. Since evaporation is a cooling process, this cooled the water in the *olla*.

Until we got the refrigerator, we used a square box enclosed with chicken wire covered with burlap which needed to be soaked several times a day to keep perishables such as meat, milk and butter cool for a day or two. The box was suspended from the rafters to keep the contents safe from ants and other crawling insects, and to allow any breeze to blow on it.

When we butchered beef, it was salted and peppered; cut with the grain into thin, quarter-inch strips; and hung on a barbed wire fence. In two or three days, this dried beef, or jerky, could be stored in sacks almost indefinitely – as they do in Mexico – as long as it was kept dry.

A delicious stew or hash was made with jerky soaked in water, then ground in a *metate* with a pestle and cooked with potatoes, onions, green chili, salt and pepper. A mouth-watering memory.

I vividly recall the women of the house back in those days ironing clothes with flatirons heated on a wood-burning stove. Around the fire box in the stove were metal tubes containing water, which when heated by the fire burning in the box, was used for baths and washing dishes.

Eventually a Kohler electric generating plant was installed. With a mere flick of the switch, it provided electricity for lights and other more modern conveniences like the new *electric* refrigerator that replaced the old Kelvinator which had played such an important part in my summer of 1944!

ARROWHEADS – 1940s

I was fortunate to grow up in the "olden days" – as my children would say – before modern civilization spread into the rough country of Arizona, New Mexico and Mexico, where Indian artifacts once abounded.

Hanging on the wall of my office is a display of 45 points, or arrowheads, in a handmade walnut frame I made in my shop as a youngster. Gathered mostly in the 1940s, my collection not only conjures up happy memories of my own childhood as I scouted for, hunted and found these treasures made hundreds, if not thousands, of years ago, but the images of those ancient peoples who made them.

When I wasn't in town going to school, I roamed six ranches in my quest for artifacts: Granddad Marion Williams' Willow Springs Ranch north of Tucson, and his San Bernardino Ranch 15 miles east of Douglas; Grandfather Ed M. Whitaker's ranch north of Fort Sumner, New Mexico, west of Alamagordo Lake (now Sumner Lake); Uncle Dell Williams' ranch in Sonora, Mexico; Dad's Rancho Las Palomas in Chihuahua; and Ezra J. Warner's ranch east of Portal, Arizona, near Rodeo, New Mexico.

On Rancho Las Palomas, there were dunes between which wind had swept the ground clear of sand leaving it as hard as concrete. One day in this particular area – perhaps an ancient ceremonial site – I found 58 points, some of chert, a flintlike quartz, while most were of obsidian, a black volcanic glass used to make beautiful arrow points, spear points, knives, tools and weapons. Tiny ones were used to hunt birds, rabbits, squirrels and other small creatures; larger ones to hunt deer, antelope, elk and bear. Some of the points I found had serrated edges resembling the retaining barbs of fishhooks…a special find.

One of the methods used to chip the chert and obsidian was to heat it, then drip cold water onto the hot stone causing it to flake. Another method was to place the obsidian or chert on a round stone or to hold it in one hand while striking it with a smaller stone or deer's antler used as a hammer or mallet.

I was indeed fortunate to grow up in the "olden days," as they provided me with a wonderful collection of points and a splendid collection of memories.

THE JAVELINA HUNT – 1945

My mental preparation for my first (and last) Javelina hunt had been underway for two weeks, and I was excited. Old John Henson had described the pigs' cave many times.

I was a boy of 16 in 1945, spending the summer at the San Bernardino Ranch; John was a widower, had a few head of cattle, and Granddad let him live there in a small wooden house in return for riding the range looking after his cattle and the fences.

My Aunt Ella and Uncle Morris Browder were leasing the ranch from Granddad. Morris had taken an early retirement from the Southern Pacific Railroad because of a bad leg.

Jack and Juana Haight came out to the ranch one weekend to visit their friends, Ella and Morris. Jack loved to hunt, and he knew there were Javelinas on the ranch. And, indeed there were.

Old John said, "Let's ride horseback up to that hill just west of the Hunt tank." The tank was an earthen dam built to catch and hold the runoff from seasonal rains to provide water for the cattle.

"We can ride around the back side of the hill, tie our horses and climb to the top of the 50-foot bluff above the pig cave. If we get there early enough, we can roll some rocks off the bluff to scare the pigs out of the cave…there's 14 or 15 of them in there."

We saddled up: John rode his own gelding, Jack rode a big bay horse of Granddad's, and I rode Brownie, Granddad's favorite fine-spirited gelding.

It was quite a ride to get to our destination seven miles away, where John said, "Get your rifles ready." He was wearing a six-shooter in a holster on his belt; Jack had a military-issue Springfield, and I had Granddad's 30-40 rifle.

Climbing to the top of the hill, we rolled some small boulders off the bluff and watched as they tumbled and crashed to the ground. Eight pigs came out. They were 100 yards away, but Jack and I started shooting. Seven more came out of the cave to see what was going on, and they just stood there while we kept shooting.

We didn't hit a single one.

"Thought you fellas wanted to shoot a pig," said John.

"We're trying…can't you see that?" But Jack and I had a bad case of "buck fever," causing our hands to shake and weakness in our knees.

"Well, if you don't hit one pretty quick, I'm going to have to kill one with my six-shooter."

Just in time, Jack shot and killed a boar.

We stumbled down the rough hill to the horses and rode around the hill to the dead pig.

"Gotta cut the musk gland out of his back quick, or the meat will taste like hell…"

I don't remember who cut that sack of musk out of the boar's back, but there was a lot of blood and a terrible stench, like skunk mixed with rotting cheese.

Javelinas stink anyway, but this was disgusting. Even worse, John and Jack decided "judiciously" that inasmuch as I weighed the least, the proper thing to do would be to tie the carcass behind my saddle over Brownie's rump to pack it home.

Brownie didn't like that idea one damn bit. He kept snorting and swinging his head from side to side trying to see what was tied on his back. He tap-danced all the way home on his tippy-toes, and I had a tough time keeping him from bucking me off, along with the pig.

Was I ever relieved when we got back to the ranch, and I'm sure Brownie was too.

We skinned out the pig, and decided to cook it. We fried some; stewed some; baked some; and boiled some; and then disposed of the whole thing. (Not even John's dogs would eat it. It was enough to gag a buzzard.)

If I live to be 100, I'll never forget that pig hunt and the ride home.

And say, if you want pig meat, buy it at the store. But that's just my "expert" opinion.

NOTE: The Collared Peccary, or Javelina, is a descendent of a large pig that lived about 25 million years ago.

HOOF-AND-MOUTH QUARANTINE – 1946-1951

On December 27, 1946, the U.S. government closed its borders to the importation of Mexican cattle because of an outbreak of hoof-and-mouth disease believed to be caused by the importation from Brazil in 1945 of a large number of Brahma bulls delivered to Sacrificios Island offshore from Veracruz, and then imported into the Republic of Mexico. The cattle were thought to be suffering from the same dreaded, fatal virus that had swept through Europe from the 1800s into the 1920s.

At the time of the quarantine, Dad owned the 286,000-acre Las Palmas Ranch, where he had 6,000 head of cattle and an additional 5,000 head under contract with Mexican ranchers. Not only did the embargo cause Dad to default on a written contract with American buyers to sell the steers for thirty-three-and-one-half cents a pound, he had to pay the default penalty of $50,000.

Although Dad's steers were eventually shipped to Juarez, Mexico, where they were butchered and canned for dog food, the canneries had not yet been built; it would be two years before the meat could be processed. Dad held the steers on the Las Palmas Ranch while fighting the U.S. government. He was convinced that the disease was not the fatal *hoof-and-mouth* virus feared by cattlemen worldwide, but *ulcerative bovine infectious stomatitis*. He was encouraged to speak on behalf of Mexican ranchers by a group of cattle growers, including Oscar Flores of Chihuahua, owner of a large ranch.

When he first contacted Dad, Flores was the Undersecretary of Agriculture for the Republic of Mexico, later becoming the governor of Chihuahua, and subsequently, Attorney General of Mexico. He knew Dad was outspoken and a fighter, and urged him to take the fight to Washington.

A hearing was held before the Committee on Agriculture, House of Representatives, 80th Congress, on December 3rd, 4th and 5th of 1947. Dad presented lengthy testimony in support of the position that the disease was actually non-fatal stomatitis. His principal opponent was Bob Kleberg, owner of the famous King Ranch in south Texas, whose position was that the disease would devastate American cattle owners if not eradicated.

Mexican and American authorities developed a program, the "sanitary rifle," calling for the killing of cloven-hoofed animals in areas designated as "already infected" or "potentially dangerous." The cattle were confiscated from their poor owners and shot, leaving the peons with no other means of support. The few head they owned provided milk, cheese, butter and beef for their families, and although they were paid for the loss by the United States, they no longer had means for providing a livelihood once this money was spent.

Many American veterinarians were hired and sent to Mexico to assist with the eradication, including a few from Tucson. Some lost their lives at the hands of furious Mexicans whose cattle and means of livelihood had been destroyed.

The American government set up and maintained a mounted "hoof- and-mouth patrol" that rode the border daily, watching for the footprints of cloven-hoofed animals which, when located, were rounded up, impounded, quarantined or destroyed.

A small wooden shack – complete with corrals for several horses – was built by the U.S. government east of the San Bernardino ranch house. It had a small kitchen and living quarters for two line riders.

Although such line camps were established all along the border in a futile attempt to keep wandering livestock from coming into the United States, elk, deer, sheep, antelope, Javelina and goats crossed whenever, wherever, as did birds flying from infected to uninfected areas.

Lime vats were built in many areas through which barefoot *campesinos* and livestock were required to walk, the caustic sludge causing burns, blisters and severe pain.

From the inception of the quarantine, Dad was in contact with elected officials in Washington, developing a close relationship with Arizona Senator Carl Hayden, chairman of the Ways and Means Committee of the U.S. Senate. Traveling to Douglas in 1948, Senator Hayden encountered Dad in the lobby of the Gadsden Hotel.

"Senator, how's everything going?"

"Ben, I'm deeply concerned about the expense of the eradication program. The original cost of the eradication program was estimated to be $30 million, but has escalated to more than $140 million in less than two years. Frankly, we cannot afford it anymore. Do you have any ideas?"

"Yes, Senator, and it would be the easiest thing in the world for you to do. You have the power to eradicate the disease with the mere stroke of a pen."

"How is that?"

"As chairman of the Ways and Means Committee, you hold the purse strings. When you return to Washington, declare that there is no more money available for the eradication program and there will be no further budgetary allocations. You'll see how quickly the problem will disappear."

On September 1, 1951, the United States Department of Agriculture announced that it was happy to report that the hoof-and-mouth disease had been eradicated in Mexico and there was no longer any need for the quarantine.

It was the first time in history a plague was cured with ink.

CHUCKWAGON "COOKIES" – 1947

In 1947, Dad owned a ranch known as Las Palmas, named after the yucca-type palms growing there. It was part of the old 2,270,000-acre Rancho Las Palomas Ranch, the largest ranch on the North American continent at that time.

Located in the state of Chihuahua, Las Palomas surrounded that part of New Mexico that juts into Mexico. Purchased by Dad and four partners in February, 1941, they contracted to buy the ranch for one million dollars, payable over five years. The contract included 16,545 head of cattle.

When the ranch was paid off, the partners decided to divide it up.

"You give me the 286,000-acre Buena Vista pasture," Dad said, "and you take the rest." Thus, Rancho Las Palmas was created.

Dad ran Mexican steers on the ranch, but in 1948, the United States imposed a hoof-and-mouth quarantine, keeping Mexican cattle out. At the time, Dad had 6,000 head of steers contracted for sale and delivery to U.S. buyers.

The contracts called for delivery of the steers to the U.S. Customs corrals at Cebolla, New Mexico, with the payment of thirty-three-and-a-half cents per pound.

Because of the embargo, Dad couldn't fulfill the contracts. Instead, he sold and delivered all 6,000 head to a cannery in Juarez, Chihuahua, where they were slaughtered and canned for dog food, along with an additional 5,000 head he'd held on other ranches. Altogether, they brought only four-and-one-half cents a pound.

During roundups, cowboys worked hard from sunup to sundown finding, gathering and driving the cattle to the shipping point.

The cowboys' bedrolls were carried in one bed wagon, while two chuckwagons were needed to feed the hands. Fifteen to twenty cowboys, one cook, and his swamper, or assistant, were assigned to each chuckwagon. The swamper did chores like gathering wood, building campfires, and peeling potatoes. A beef was always butchered to provide meat for the cowboys, a welcome addition to their usual diet of tortillas and beans.

My favorites were the chuckwagon "cookies" – fresh, soft biscuits six inches in diameter and one inch thick. These were baked in a Dutch oven over the campfire until golden brown, then dipped in warm *piloncillo* syrup (brown unrefined sugar) - the best chuckwagon cookies ever made.

On one particular occasion, one of the cooks didn't show up. The last thing a cowboy wants to do is cook, but one of the men had to be selected by lot and assigned the job. It was understood, however, that if anybody complained about the food, the complainer would automatically become the cook.

About three or four days into the roundup, the substitute cook grew disgusted with his assignment and thought he would do something to cause the men to complain. He over-salted the beans. Nobody complained. He burned the breakfast bacon. Nobody complained.

Early one morning, before the cowboys got up, he went to the line where the horses were tethered and gathered a handful of "horse apples." He then made a "stew" and served it to the men when they returned for supper. Several of the men tasted the stew, looked at each other, and scowled.

Another cowboy groaned, "Good God, this tastes like horse s..., uh, apples," and quickly added, "but aren't they delicious?"

Trap set, sprung, failed. Those cowboys REALLY hated to cook.

A CRASH COURSE – 1947

In the summer of 1947, when I was 18 years old, Dad took me to his ranch in the state of Chihuahua, west of Juarez, Mexico. He called the ranch Las Palmas (the palms).

He put me in charge of making sure the cattle had water and salt, a big job, as the ranch was large – 286,000 acres, or nearly 45 sections. Many of the wells had gasoline engines and pump jacks which pumped water when there was no wind to turn the windmill fans. It would be my job to service them.

Benjamín Sandoval was assigned to be my companion. Benjamín and I were *tocayos* (same name).

Dad's native language was Spanish as he was born in Mexico and learned to speak it before he learned English, but he never spoke it at home. I spoke only a smattering of Spanish, even though I had studied it in Douglas High School. Imagine my surprise when Dad and I arrived at the ranch and he gathered the men to say, "This is my son, Ben. If any of you speak English, you are not to speak it to him. I want him to learn Spanish, so speak to him only in Spanish. Understand?"

Well, this was like casting me into the water, saying "Sink or swim!" But, I tried.

Dad provided me with his Jeep – the first civilian Jeep to come into southern Arizona after World War II. I was driving alone one day when it stalled half-a-mile

Las Palmas Ranch

from headquarters. I walked to the house where I got a large truck and a Mexican cowboy to go back with me to recover the Jeep. Benjamín was not at the headquarters at the time. He had gone home to Janos to visit his family.

Parking the truck in front of the Jeep, I fastened a heavy chain between the two vehicles, and asked, "*Puede hacerlo?*" (Can you do it?)

I wish now that I'd known how to ask, "Do you know how to drive the truck and pull me back to the ranch?"

"*Pues, si.*" (Of course.)

I told him in my best new Spanish that I would steer the Jeep and he was to pull me to headquarters.

As he climbed into the truck and I mounted

Author at Las Palmas Ranch, 1948

the Jeep, I shouted, "*Bueno, vamos.*" (Come on, let's go.)

Whereupon he shifted the truck into reverse, gunned the engine, and smashed into the front of the Jeep, crumbling the hood, radiator and headlights.

"No, dammit, forward gear!"

He understood my yelling, changed gears and we headed for the ranch house, thus ending my "crash course" in Spanish 101.

Author in front of his 1948 Chevrolet coupe at Las Palmas Ranch

MY LITTLE FLOWER – 1947

After graduating from New Mexico Military Institute in Roswell and entering the University of Arizona in 1947, I found college life to be exciting after the rigid discipline and closely-supervised life of a cadet.

In those days, "Greek" fraternities were "in," and after going through rush week, I pledged Sigma Nu. In the spring, our house held an exchange dinner with the Delta Gamma sorority. A few of our men would go to their house, and some of the girls would come to our house, where I had been selected to help host the visitors.

We exchanged pleasantries and then were called to dinner, where I was seated across from a cute auburn-haired gal with hazel eyes. When it was my turn to introduce myself, I said, "My name is Ben Williams and I'm from Douglas." To which the pretty young lady exclaimed, "You're Ben Williams? Your laundry is in my room!"

"And please, pray tell, how is it that my clothes are in your room?"

"I am Flo Sharpe's roommate and she is from Douglas, and we live in Yuma Hall where your laundry has been for some time!"

I explained that Flo's mother, Edith, and my mother, Dot, and I had an arrangement whereby every couple of weeks, Flo would take or send her laundry and my laundry home to be laundered. Then it would be my turn…thus my clothes were in Daisy's bedroom. We laughed.

We visited and I learned that she was from Prescott, and had transferred to the university from Mount St. Marys in Los Angeles. Then, some of the brothers suggested we all go dancing at the Double RRs on east Speedway. (It is known as the Bashful Bandit nowadays, and patronized by motorcyclists.)

At the end of the evening, I took Daisy to Yuma Hall in my canary-yellow Pontiac convertible, picked up my laundry, and said goodnight.

Being completely enchanted by the cute little miss, I wondered, *how am I going to snag her? She didn't seem too interested in me. Perhaps if I don't call her for a while, there's a chance she may be curious as to why I have not called.*

Three weeks went by. I finally broke down and invited her to go to a movie at the old Fox Theatre downtown. After the movie, we went to the Desert Inn drive-in for a soda.

One thing led to another, one date led to another, and after a "whirlwind" courtship of *four long years*, Daisy and I were married in the garden at the Lodge on the Desert on Alvernon, by Robert Tullar, Superior Court judge, on June 2, 1951.

It was there I gave Daisy the nickname, "My Little Flower." And now, four wonderful children and six loving grandchildren later, Daisy is, was, and always will be "My Little Flower."

THE METER DOES NOT LIE – 1950s

Granddad and Nana lived for many years at 1305 Eleventh Street in Douglas, Arizona. They had a nice, modest, comfortable three-bedroom home. In the back yard, Nana had a greenhouse in which she grew vegetables and flowers. Her tomatoes, zucchini, radishes, lettuce, onions and chilis were without equal. The salsa she made was the finest.

One day in the early 1950s, Granddad noticed that his water bill had sky-rocketed to nearly 10 times what it normally ran. He called the City of Douglas Water Department. They came out, examined the meter and informed him they could not find any leaks and that the reading was correct. They suggested that he hire a plumber to check for leaks on his side of the meter. He did just that, and the plumber told him that he could not find any leaks. The next month, the water bill arrived and was again nearly 10 times normal. Granddad called the City of Douglas Water Department, and again complained that there was something wrong as the bill was too high.

The city sent out a crew to re-check the meter reading and to see if there was anything wrong with the meter itself, and again found nothing.

Granddad grudgingly paid the bill.

When the following month's bill arrived, it was again outrageously high. Granddad angrily called the City of Douglas Water Department and complained.

"Mr. Williams, we have checked your water meter twice. We have sent crews out to check to see if everything is working all right. *We can find nothing wrong.* If you don't pay the bill, we are going to cut your water off. Also, Mr. Williams, there is something we want you to know."

"What is that?"

"Mr. Williams, the meter does not lie."

With that, Granddad paid the bill, and for about a year continued to pay the high water bills.

One day he noticed that the bills had fallen off to the minimum. *This is wonderful. They've fixed the problem.*

Nana continued to grow her flowers and vegetables, and eight months went by.

One day Granddad received a call from the City of Douglas Water Department: "Mr. Williams, we have noticed that your water bill has fallen down to the minimum in the last eight months."

"That's right, and I've been paying the bill every month."

"Well, there's something wrong. The meter's got to be broken. We're going to average the bills for the past 18 months and then bill you for that average to catch up."

"That's not right. I'm not going to pay it."

"Well, Mr. Williams, if you don't pay the bill, we're going to cut your water off and sue you for that average."

"Before you do that, I want you to know one thing."

"What is that, Mr. Williams?"

"I'm not going to pay any more than what the meter reads and you can darn well sue until the cows come home…and you'd better not cut my water off. Remember one thing — *the meter does not lie.*"

WONDER EAR – 1950s

In the early 1950s, while serving on active duty with the United States Army Tank Corps, I suffered a hearing loss, as did many other soldiers exposed to artillery and the loud noise of the tank cannon, or "tubes," as we tankers called them. Neither earplugs nor cotton balls were thought of in those days as protection for one's hearing.

My hearing loss turned out to be permanent, and over a period of years had grown progressively worse.

Being an attorney, a profession in which hearing is essential, I tried numerous hearing aids of different types and models. None were satisfactory and most were exorbitantly priced.

During his lifetime, my father perfected and patented a number of ideas including a rotary pump and rotary engine. As I pondered the problems with my hearing, the natural family bent for inventiveness surfaced, and a thought came to me. Thoughts can be patented if unique, and mine was for a new type of hearing aid which I set about to construct.

To make a working model, I selected a piece of brilliant mother-of-pearl from an abalone shell, from which I cut a 1/16th-inch-by-1-inch disk. I drilled two small holes in the disk to use to attach a connector and a safety pin-like clasp to secure the device.

I carefully selected a 14" piece of white silk cord, into which I wove three strands of fine gold thread, as gold is brilliant and does not tarnish or oxidize. I then cut a smaller disk approximately the size of a thumbnail that would easily fit into my ear. I carefully affixed one end of the silk and gold cord to the large disk, to which I had attached a gold safety pin. This pin didn't need to be gold, but it was best to use brass or another shiny metal.

I carefully fastened the other end of the silk and gold cord to the small button and then placed the small button in my ear canal and pinned the larger disk to my lapel. It is essential that these be placed on one's outer clothing for maximum effectiveness, and it is best to have the silk and gold cord draped across the chest of the user's body.

I found this device to be more satisfactory than any other hearing aids I had tried, for as I approached people, they could tell immediately that I was hard-of-hearing and would shout so I could hear them!

I named my device the "Wonder Ear," not to be confused with Miracle Ear, a well-known hearing aid, and submitted the required drawings and a prototype model of "Wonder Ear" to the U. S. Patent Office.

It has been more than 50 years, and I cannot imagine why I have not heard from the Patent Office with their approval of my Wonder Ear.

Perhaps they too have developed a "deaf ear."

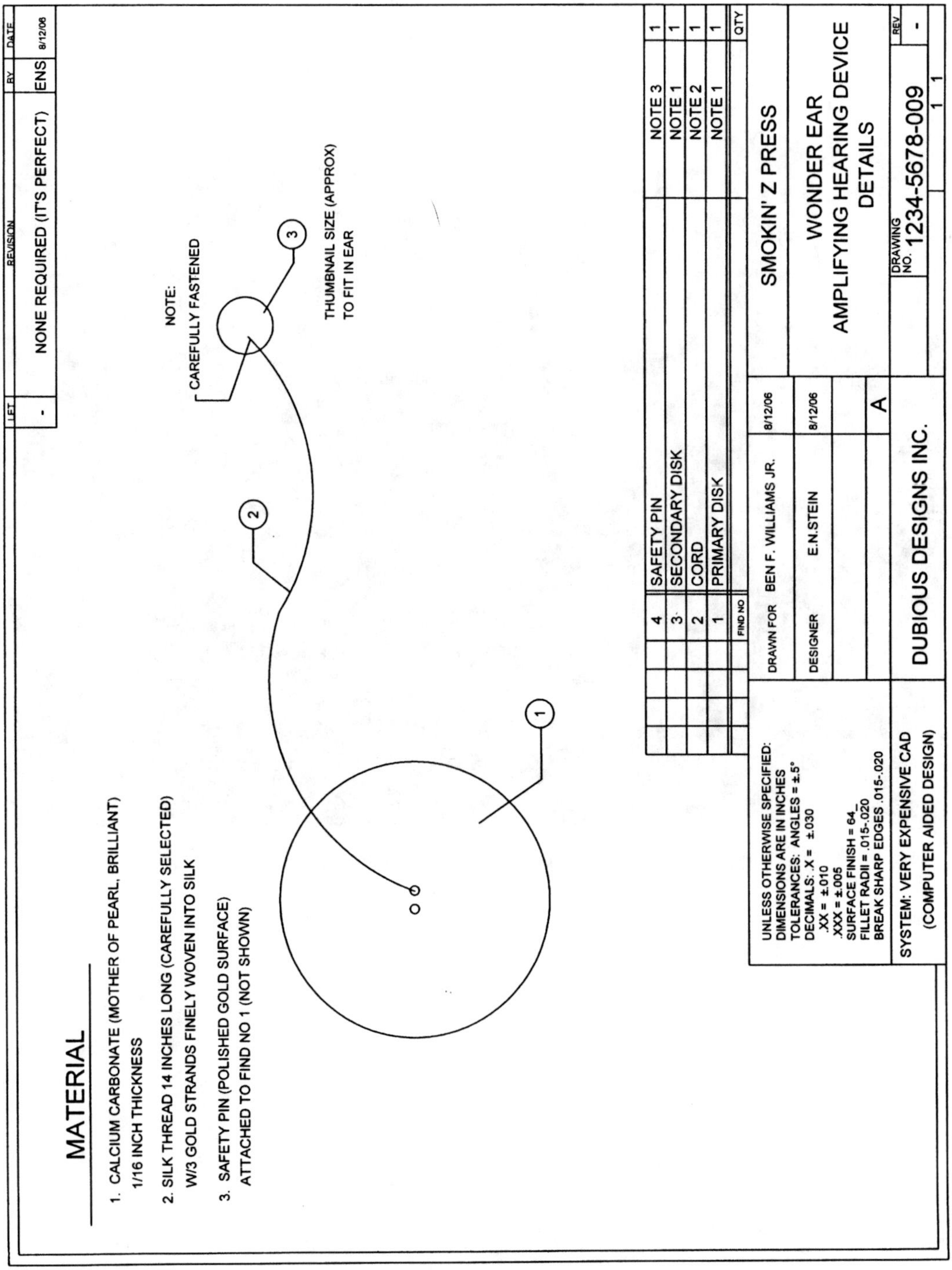

Engineer's drawing of invention

Mill site - La Gloria tungsten mine in wilds of Sonora

MY 30-30 CARBINE – 1950s

"Give me your rifle, Mr. Williams," demanded the Mexican federal officer.

In the late 1950s, Dad owned *La Gloria*, a tungsten mine in Mexico, on the banks of the Yaqui River in Sonora.

When I began practicing law in 1956, Dad and I officed together in the Gadsden Hotel, although he was not a lawyer. When he was down at the mine 135 miles south of the border, our only means of communication was by shortwave radio. We discussed family matters, world events, and the price of tungsten on the stock market, as well as what supplies, building materials and personal items he needed to have shipped down by truck.

Early on, he asked to borrow my Winchester 30-30 carbine rifle for his employees to use. They supplemented their basic diet of *frijoles*, tortillas and occasional cans of tomatoes and green beans with the wild turkey and deer they shot using my dandy saddle gun.

One day, a Mexican federal officer appeared at the mine, demanding to speak to my father.

"I know you have a rifle in camp," he said. "Show me your permit." After the Mexican revolution, it was next to impossible to get permits to own guns legally.

"I don't have a permit."

"Give me your rifle, Mr. Williams. I'm confiscating it, for in Mexico it is a violation of the law to have a rifle without a permit."

"If you feel you must, officer, but first, I want to assemble my men. It will take only ten minutes to get them here. Then," he continued, "I want you to explain to all 80 of them why you must take the rifle they use to provide their meat."

The officer was silent for a moment. "Mr. Williams," he said, "on second thought, I don't believe I'll take the rifle now. I'll take it the next time I am here."

The officer left and never returned, but I lost my 30-30 carbine after all. As they say in the mining business, somebody "high-graded" it.

Ben F. Williams, Sr. at Nacori Chico on his way to La Gloria

AN URGENT MATTER – 1956

After serving two years in the Army Tank Corps and three years in law school at the University of Arizona, I returned to Douglas with my wife, Daisy, in the fall of 1956. I had passed the Arizona Bar exam and was admitted and eager to begin my practice.

I opened an office in the Gadsden Hotel where – it was rumored – Pancho Villa had ridden his horse up the Italian marble staircase leading to the mezzanine and where a chip remains in the seventh stair as evidence of his famous ride.

Dad and I officed together. He was not a lawyer, but always seemed to need a lawyer's services. The rent was right, for Dad paid it, providing me with a dandy place for my new law practice. The Gadsden Hotel was the social and business center of Douglas, with a famous coffee shop, fine food and a fancy lobby where clients could wait in comfort. This was a good thing, as our office was quite small.

Daisy and I moved into my maternal grandparents' house at 1909 Ninth Street. They had recently moved to Midland, Texas, to wind up my grandfather Ed Whitaker's law practice of many years. Daisy and I and our daughters, Elizabeth and Diane, found the Whitaker home to be large and comfortable for our small family, and again, the rent was right. We had only to pay the equivalent of the real estate taxes.

Rosie Pavlovich, my legal secretary, was a wonderful assistant, having worked for Bob Morrison, the former Arizona Attorney General. I was fortunate to find someone of her caliber to work in Douglas, although she and her husband, Lou Pavlovich, lived in Bisbee, where he was the editor of the *Bisbee Daily Review*, Bisbee's main newspaper. Rosie commuted 46 miles each day.

One day Rosie said, "Your paper boy, Johnny Plinski, has made an appointment to see you today. He won't tell me why he needs to talk to you, but he says it's urgent and confidential. He will be here at two o'clock."

Johnny Plinski was 10 years old, lived across the street from us and delivered the *Douglas Daily Dispatch* to us faithfully every day. When he appeared promptly at two o'clock and was shown into my office, he asked, "Do you mind if I close the door?"

"Please come in and close it. So what's your problem, Johnny?"

"Well, my mom caught me smoking this morning and she's going to tell my dad, who will whip me when he comes home from work. Can you get an injunction for me, Mr. Williams, so Dad won't punish me?"

"I don't believe I can help you, Johnny. An injunction is usually issued in order to prevent an irreparable injury from happening."

"I know, Mr. Williams, and that's why I've come to you. When my father comes home tonight, an irreparable injury will happen to me…it's for sure I'll get a terrible lickin'…"

"I'm sorry, Johnny, I can't help you…"

"Don't worry about your fee…I'll pay it out of my earnings from my paper route."

"Johnny, you're just going to have to take the punishment. You know, smoking is not good for you anyway."

"I know," he said. "I just found that out."

When Rosie told her husband, Lou, about Johnny's problem, he wrote a story about it, putting it on the UPI wire. It went all over the world. I even received clippings of the story from the European edition of *Stars and Stripes*.

I never did hear what happened to Johnny that night, nor did I ever learn where Johnny had heard about injunctions.

LA GLORIA – 1956

In 1956, while Dad and I were officing in the Gadsden Hotel, he acquired *La Gloria*, a tungsten property in San Mateo, Sonora, Mexico, by the Yaqui River, 135 miles south of the border in wild, remote and rugged country. Always interested in mining ventures, Dad knew the value of tungsten as it was classified as a critical metal by our military. Tungsten was used for incandescent lamp filaments, contact points, and, most important, the hardening of steel in armor-piercing ordnance.

However, in order to own a mine in Mexico, there had to be a valid Mexican corporation, and in order to have a valid Mexican corporation, there had to be at least five incorporators, all Mexican citizens. With the help of Santiago Campbell, a notary public in Agua Prieta, a corporation was formed: "*Minerales America, S.A.*"

The mining concession was transferred to the name of Minerales America; stock was issued to Dad, with nominal shares for Mexican citizens designated by him to be the shareholders. These Mexican incorporators gave their promissory – albeit fictitious – notes for substantial amounts of money, and, through means of an instrument, pledged their stock as security for repayment of the "loans," thus circumventing Mexican laws concerning foreign owners of mining companies.

As there were no roads except for the dangerous four-wheeled vehicle trail from Sahuaripa, nearly three hours south of the mine, Dad had his crews build a 52-mile stretch of road from Divisaderos, Mexico, to the mine.

Requiring large quantities of dynamite to blast through solid rock, the road was difficult and expensive to build, but necessary. When finished, it was used by the heavy trucks hauling milled tungsten concentrate to Douglas, and building materials and supplies back to the mine. Except during rainy season when the road was washed out or impassable, the trip took at least seven hours each way.

Dad had his crews scrape an airstrip on the side of a hill four miles southeast of the mine for small aircraft to use for quick trips or emergencies. I was lucky enough to make one trip to La Gloria when Bill Curtis flew his Cessna-172 down with much-needed supplies.

That night, Dad took me out to the side of the mountain where the original owners, the *campesinos*, had discovered the outcroppings of tungsten and superficially mined, or "picked," several deposits. Using Dad's black light, we were able to determine the presence of tungsten because of the glowing bluish-white fluorescence emanating from scheelite, a mineral found in combination with tungsten.

Being in virgin country, everything had to be built from the ground up: living quarters to accommodate the mine and mill workers and the cooks and swampers who maintained the camp; a small wooden office building; and Dad's headquarters – two bedrooms with cooking facilities.

All supplies, equipment and building materials, including lumber, nails, tools, cement, roofing, cable, rope, dynamite, electric generators and compressors, were trucked to the four-building settlement of Badesi on the north side of the Yaqui River. From there they were ferried to the south side of the river by *pongo*, a heavy raft guided by thick, overhead, 100-yard cables suspended from opposite river banks.

The process was reversed when the 20-kilo bags of concentrate were ferried to waiting trucks, loaded and shipped to Douglas where they were reloaded into railroad cars for delivery to east-and-west-coast buyers.

When Dad was down at the isolated La Gloria mine, we communicated by using his clandestine shortwave radio – clandestine in that it was not licensed by the Mexican Federal Communications Commission. Promptly at 1:15 every afternoon, I went across the border to Agua Prieta to the home of Alfredo Villascuesa, manager of the local branch of Banco de Nogales. Alfredo used his shortwave radio

Pongo used to cross Yaqui River to La Gloria mine

primarily to communicate with his bank headquarters in Hermosillo. As Dad's company, Minerales America, S.A., was a customer of his bank, Alfredo graciously let us use his legal radio.

Other than being able to hear only one or two Mexican commercial radio stations, Dad had no other means of communication. We discussed materials and supplies he needed for the mine and mill, for his employees, and for himself, like the occasional bottle of Johnny Walker Black Label scotch. I gave Dad the market news, the spot price of tungsten, the latest world and current events, and family news.

Tungsten concentrate contains an impurity, bismuth, used, for example, in Pepto Bismol. A large, beautiful and expensive electromagnetic separator was purchased by the company, and installed in a building in Agua Prieta for the purpose of removing the bismuth. It failed, and the concentrate continued to be sold on the world market at a discount.

A major U.S. corporation, Union Carbide, became interested in La Gloria, sending their geologists to examine the property with the idea of buying it. Our inability to separate the bismuth from the concentrate was an ongoing, frustrating problem. It was hoped that Union Carbide would be able to overcome the difficulty and produce a purer, high grade concentrate.

"How much do you want for La Gloria, Mr. Williams, including the pongo and all improvements?"

"Two million dollars, cash."

The price seemed satisfactory, and the company's lawyers from Mexico City came to Douglas, where Licenciado Erasmo Lozano Rocha from Cananea, and I, representing Minerales America, began negotiating a contract for the sale.

Ben F. Williams, Sr., James Douglas (son of "Rawhide" Jimmy Douglas, brother of Lewis Douglas, U.S. Ambassador to the Court of St. James during FDR's administration) and Mrs. Douglas, shown in cut of road built from Divisaderos, Sonora, to La Gloria mine

After several weeks of drafting and redrafting the contract, it was in a form acceptable to both buyer and seller. It was then sent to the corporate offices of Union Carbide in New York City for review.

Minerales America received word that the contract was to be presented to the board of directors on May 15, 1958...with a green light from the Union Carbide management team to "buy."

On May 13, 1958, two days before the meeting, Vice-President Nixon's motorcade was stoned by political activists while on an official visit to Caracas, Venezuela. Nixon had been traveling in the U.S. Embassy's automobile, and as a result of the stoning, a great political uproar was heard throughout the world via newspapers, radio and television.

Confronted with this new development, the board of directors of Union Carbide refused to go ahead with the acquisition of La Gloria. In addition, they adopted a resolution establishing a policy precluding any investments in any Latin American countries, including Mexico.

The deal was dead, and the feasibility of the continued operation of the La Gloria mine was examined by Minerales America, S.A. It was determined that it would be best to sell the property to a group of Mexican investors, who purchased the entire operation and all improvements, including the machinery and equipment, all of which was removed and sold, and the buildings cannibalized.

That close to a "home run" for Minerales America, S.A., La Gloria proved – like so many other mining ventures – to be an "out"…but what a glorious ride!

GUILTY OR NOT – 1959

In June of 1959, Luke Carter, a man accused of theft, asked me to defend him. When I asked why he had chosen me, he said, "There was a note on the jail wall – Ben Williams - Good Lawyer - Telephone 364-4418."

Luke was a white male, 6'2" tall, raw-boned and well-tanned. He wore a three-inch scar on his left cheek, which he said he'd received after he quit school, having finished only the eighth grade. "My folks kicked me out of the house and told me I was on my own. I was 18, the oldest of six kids."

Most – or at least many – persons accused of crimes say they were framed, and Luke was no exception. He was a construction worker and had been accused by his boss of stealing tools and materials worth $2,500 from the job site. The Cochise County Attorney had charged Luke with grand theft, a felony.

I talked with Luke at great length to learn the facts of the case. He acted like he was "set upon" by the accuser and the investigating officers and insisted, "I didn't do anything" – a story I had heard many times.

I told my client that my fee would be $5,000 if I got him off. He agreed, but said he would have to pay me after the trial and that he could borrow the money from a friend after he got free. Business had been slow, so I agreed to represent him, and set out to do my job.

I studied the law carefully and decided which witnesses I would call. In trials today, there is not much chance of surprise testimony because of the extensive pretrial preparation, depositions, interrogatories, and interviews of witnesses, but in those days, we went through little pretrial discovery.

The day arrived for the trial, and we proceeded to the Cochise County Courthouse in Bisbee. I had requested a jury.

The judge drew 24 names for the jury panel. The attorneys were permitted to ask questions of each juror, a procedure known as *voir dire,* whereby the defendant and the State could question each person to determine whether or not he or she would be a good juror for the case.

The plaintiff and the defendant were each permitted six "peremptory" challenges, meaning they could challenge a juror for any reason whatsoever, or for no reason, such as not liking the color of his hair, or her eyes.

I disqualified two witnesses, and the prosecution challenged one. After the jury was selected and empaneled, the judge asked, "Gentlemen, are you ready to proceed with trial?"

The State announced ready, and I declared ready for the defendant, whereupon the State presented its case and rested.

I put on Luke's case and rested.

The county attorney and I delivered our closing arguments. The judge gave instructions to the jury, outlining the applicable law that should be considered when determining – beyond a reasonable doubt – whether the defendant is guilty of committing the crime of which he is accused.

As the jury retired to deliberate, the judge and lawyers went to the Elks' Club for a stiff drink or two.

We had only downed a couple of drinks when the bailiff called the judge at the club to say that the jury was in, whereupon court and counsel returned to the courtroom.

The judge asked the foreman if a verdict had been reached. "Yes, your Honor."

"What is your verdict?"

"Not guilty, your Honor."

As we left the courthouse, Luke turned to me and said, "You know, until I heard your argument and the jury's verdict, I thought I was guilty!"

HERE COME DE JUDGE – 1960s

Raúl Castro and his wife, Pat, owned a horse (Shetland pony) farm in Tucson at River Road and Dodge Boulevard. Raúl was a Pima County Superior Court judge at the time, and in later years, shared this story with me.

It seems that on weekends, Pat would put a list of chores on the refrigerator for Raúl to do so he would have his weekend work cut out for him.

One Saturday morning, Raúl, dressed in Levis, boots, an old shirt and a straw hat, was painting the white picket fence that enclosed their 40-acre farm.

Midmorning, a United States Border Patrol vehicle was driving by. When the officers saw Raúl painting, they stopped and beckoned to him, saying in Spanish, "*Oyes! Tu, vente aquí.*" (Hey, you, come here.)

"*Quién, yo?*" (Who, me?)

"*Si, tu!*"

Raúl approached the officers and one asked, "*Como te llamas?*" (What's your name?)

"*Me llamo Castro.*"

The officer asked, "*Tienes tarjeta verde?*" (Do you have a green card?)

"*No, Señor.*"

"*Qué estás haciendo aquí?*" (What are you doing here?)

"*Trabajando.*" (Working.)

"*Con quién estás trabajando?*" (Who are you working for?)

"*Para la Señora.* (For the lady.)

"*Qué está pagándote?"* (What is she paying you?)

"*No me paga."* (She doesn't pay me.)

"*Pues, porqué estás trabajando?* (Then, why are you working?)

Whereupon, Raúl responded in perfect English, "Because she lets me sleep with her."

Too late, the patrolmen noticed the sign over the gate: CASTRO HORSE FARM. Stricken, he asked "Are you Raúl H. Castro, the Superior Court judge?"

"You better believe I am."

"Our mistake, Judge Castro. Please excuse the intrusion. We must be going now…have a good day."

Which he did…and laughs every time he remembers the incident of the mistaken identity.

SHE BELONGS TO ME – 1960s

A Mexican lady presented herself at my office in the Gadsden Hotel in the early 1960s. She could not speak English, so we conversed in Spanish.

She told me a sad tale of how her husband, Bill, beat and slapped her, and asked if there was anything she could do about it. She was from Mexico and was married to an American man. They lived alone on a remote ranch northeast of Douglas. She said she was not an American citizen, but was living in the United States legally.

I explained that under the laws of Arizona, a husband has no right to inflict harm on a spouse, and that such action would constitute physical cruelty, and was grounds for divorce. She seemed surprised. "You mean I can get a divorce and he can no longer beat me?"

"That's right," I said. I asked her if she had any place to go when we filed for divorce because she should not return to the ranch where for sure her husband would inflict more serious physical harm. She said she had a sister with whom she could stay until the divorce was granted.

I prepared a complaint for divorce, she signed it, and I filed it in the Cochise County Superior Court. I told her not to return to the ranch, but to stay with her sister, which she did.

About three days later I heard a terrible ruckus in my outer office. "I want to talk to Williams."

My secretary said, "I'm sorry. Mr. Williams is busy right now, sir. May I have your name?"

"No. Where is Williams?"

"I'm sorry, he's busy."

I stepped out of my office and said, "I'm Ben Williams. How may I help you?"

"My name is Bill Snow, and you filed a divorce against me."

"That's right, Mr. Snow. I understand you have been beating your wife, and she does not want to live with you any longer. As a matter of fact, she wants a divorce."

"She can't get a divorce," he roared. "She's mine!"

"No way," I said.

"You'd better believe she's mine," he said, and whipping out his wallet, he produced a receipt signed by the madam of the Silver Dollar. "Here's proof. I paid $200 for her over in Agua Prieta, and she's mine. I bought and paid for her, cash. No way in hell can she get a divorce. I own her."

"Indeed she can divorce you," I said, "and she's going to."

I took Mrs. Snow to Bisbee after the appropriate number of days had expired. She got her divorce, and I never heard another word from either of them.

The "snow" job was over.

PERCY'S LIE DETECTOR – 1961

I was appointed City Attorney of Douglas on June 1, 1961, because Dr. Joe S. Causey, Mayor, broke the tied vote cast by his Democratic city council.

One fine morning in July, I headed for a court hearing in the Justice Court of Cochise County, Precinct Number Two. It was to be held in City Hall where the bench and courtroom were shared by George W. Martin, J.P., and Henry Elvey, City Magistrate. The City Clerk's office and the City Council chambers were on the second floor, while Chief of Police Percy Bowden's office was on the first floor on the left as one entered the building from Tenth Street.

Bowden was the longest tenured chief of police in the United States. He joined the police force in 1918, and with the exception of a two-year break when Mayor Millard Haymore was in office, he continued to serve until 1971.

A dyed-in-the-wool Democrat and political wheelhorse for his party, Bowden had great influence in the affairs of city government and in the selection of elected and appointed city officials. One exception was the two-year term of a Republican, my father, who was mayor from 1948 to 1950.

Percy Bowden was known for getting things done in an expeditious and effective manner, making Douglas a fine, crime-free community in which to live. On that particular morning in July, I was to witness his techniques first-hand.

As I walked past Percy's office, I noticed a boy about eight years old sitting in a chair next to his desk. In each hand, the boy was holding a bare wire attached to the bells of an old-fashioned alarm clock, which, when the alarm went off, were struck by a clapper. The boy was terrified.

Seeing me in the doorway, Chief Bowden volunteered, "Hello, Mr. Williams. It seems youngsters are causing trouble, and I'm going to get to the bottom of these problems. They've been knocking over garbage cans, marking sidewalks with paint and crayons, riding bicycles on people's lawns and letting the air out of people's tires. It is my intention today to determine who the leader is and the names of the members of the gang. We are going to stamp out all this monkey business once and for all."

Of course, the youngster heard the chief's words, which added to his fright.

"What's that on your desk, Chief?" I asked.

"It's a lie detector." He had rigged the clock so he could ring the bells himself by tripping a wire. "If he tells a lie, the bells will ring. If he tells the truth, the bells won't ring."

I had just entered the courtroom to hear my case, when I heard the sound of bells, and on my way out of city hall, I stopped by Percy's office.

"Did your lie detector work, Chief?"

"Yes, the young fellow confessed to everything. He gave me the names of the ring leader and all the gang members. We're not going to have any more trouble after I talk to them."

Perhaps Percy Bowden's machine was a little before its time; perhaps it was not as sophisticated as modern lie detectors are, but I believe it was far more effective because it actually resulted in a confession.

COSTLY PERFUME

I got a call one day from Susie Krentz. She and her husband, Rob, own a ranch 35 miles east of Douglas in the same valley as the San Bernardino Ranch once owned by my grandfather, Marion Williams.

What prompted Susie's call was her inquiry into the history of the "Z" livestock brand which now belongs to me. I told her that when Granddad bought the ranch from John Slaughter's widow in 1937, the brand came with the ranch, and that Slaughter first registered it in Arizona in 1915.

Susie and I discussed range conditions, rainfall, and the price of beef. Then she said, "We had a skunk problem last month."

"What happened?"

"Well, while Rob and I were gone to church one Saturday afternoon, the kitchen door on the side of the house blew open. When we got back, we closed the door, had supper and went to bed.

"Rob got up early the next morning to get ready to ride the water line to be sure the cattle had water. I was sort of snoozing when there was a terrible ruckus under our bed. There was hissing and snarling, and all of a sudden Roger, our 15-year-old cat, came bounding across the bed. Our kids named him after Roger Rabbit of comic fame...but this wasn't funny. He smelled awful. The whole room smelled awful.

"All I could see when I looked under the bed were two shiny eyes. I hollered for Rob. He came running with his 22 rifle with the scope. When he crouched under the bed to shoot the skunk, it was too dark to see through his scope, so he had to run out and get his other 22. When he shot the skunk, the whole place stunk to high heaven."

"How did you get it out from under the bed.?"

"We took the mattress off the bed, put the skunk in a bucket, took it outside and left it in the desert…away from the house."

"How did you clean up the mess?"

"We took all the clothes out of the closets and put them in the horse trailer outside. He'd always promised me a walk-in closet, but that was not what I had in mind.

"We asked around and were told that a good scrubbing with hydrogen peroxide and baking soda might help deodorize everything. It worked on the clothes, bedding and kitchen stuff, but the carpet in the whole house had to be replaced. We scrubbed all the furniture we'd put out in the yard, but we had to buy new drapes and mattresses. And, worst of all, the whole inside of the house had to be repainted.

"Poor Roger smelled so bad we couldn't get near him, so we gave him a bath. That old cat had never had a bath and he darn near croaked going through his first one of hydrogen peroxide and baking soda. Even though we got most of the smell out of his hair, he still smells mighty strong.

"Rob and I slept on a pallet in the living room for a few weeks until we could tolerate moving back into our bedroom.

"And then one night, we saw a skunk coming around the corner of the house. There was a whole family of skunks living under the porch. We set Havaheart traps, caught them all, and are skunk-free at last!"

"How much did all of this cost you, Susie?"

"Close to $10,000," she answered ruefully. "It was mighty costly perfume."

And speaking of skunks…

THE SKUNK SHOW – 1962

In 1962, I was City Attorney for "The Town Too Tough To Die," Tombstone, Arizona, population 1,504. On the third Wednesday of each month, as prescribed by the city charter, I motored to Tombstone from Douglas to attend the council meeting.

The mayor, council, city clerk, supporting staff and I met in the clerk's office in the city hall one hour before the meeting. The clerk's office was on the ground floor next to the fire station, in the same building. Meetings began promptly at 8:00 p.m. It was the custom of the mayor and council to go over the agenda to make sure there were no items that might come up and surprise the council during the meeting.

The council chambers were on the second story of the building. If the meeting did not start promptly at 8:00, the audience upstairs would stamp their feet on the wooden floor, causing thunderous noise. Tom Pitcher, the mayor, would then say, "The natives are getting restless...we'd better go up and start the meeting."

In those days there was little to do in Tombstone; there was not even a movie theater. Council meetings provided the highest form of entertainment for the citizenry, and the house was always packed, nary a chair was empty, with standing room only along the walls.

The Tombstone charter, one of the oldest in the state of Arizona, dates back to 1881. Everything had to be approved by the mayor and council, including such things as applications for permits.

A man claiming to be a grandson of the great Apache chief, Cochise, made application for a "pet skunk show" for which he wanted to charge admission.

The item was put on the agenda, and at the proper time the mayor called for its consideration by the council.

Chief Cochise's grandson brought with him two cages, each of which contained a skunk. Addressing the council, he informed us that the skunks had undergone surgery to remove their musk glands. As he put it, "These skunks are absolutely and unconditionally safe and odor-free."

That evening he was dressed in his finest, wearing a nicely-washed and neatly-pressed white shirt. One of the council members asked, "Are you sure those skunks are safe?"

"You bet," the Indian said, reaching into the cage to remove a large skunk. "I'll show you how safe these skunks are."

He raised the black-and-white animal high above his head and shook it vigorously. Terrified, the skunk let go the biggest bowel movement ever seen – all over the Indian's snowy-white shirt.

The crowd roared with laughter. A council member made a motion, which was quickly seconded and carried. The "pet skunk show" permit was granted, but none too soon.

MURDER ONE – 1962

While sitting in the Cochise County Superior Court during a routine Monday calendar call in June of 1962, I was jolted out of my mental doldrums by the Honorable Raúl H. Castro, when, in response to the clerk's call of the case *State of Arizona v. Pedro Cruz*, number C7642, I heard the judge say, "It is ordered that Ben Williams be and he is hereby appointed to represent the defendant Pedro Cruz in this case. Being that it is a capital case, I feel that the defendant should have two attorneys to defend him. Therefore, I also appoint Dale Fenter as co-counsel to Mr. Williams."

Dale had just entered the courtroom and was as surprised by his appointment as I was by mine. Cruz had been found to be indigent and was therefore entitled to have a court-appointed lawyer. Dale and I had no choice in the matter. As officers of the court, we were obligated, once appointed, to give the defendant the best possible defense whether he was guilty or not.

We went to the Cochise County jail on the top floor of the courthouse where the jailer showed us into the interrogation room. He then brought Cruz into the room and left.

Dale was raised on a ranch near Greaterville, Arizona, where, as a boy, he rode his horse to the one-room schoolhouse, the place of learning for grades one through eight. With all the Hispanic and Anglo kids in this environment, Dale learned to speak fluent Spanish. I was raised on the Mexican border at Douglas in an Anglo-Hispanic culture, which educated me to the Spanish language as well. Cruz spoke a smattering of English but was more comfortable speaking in his native Spanish tongue.

We interviewed Cruz, who was now sober, having been in jail for 72 hours. No bond was set, it being a capital case (punishable by death). Cruz was little help, having committed the crime while drunk. He remembered nothing of murdering his daughter. After talking to him for half-an-hour and learning nothing, I said, "Let's file a motion asking the court to order a physical and psychiatric examination for our client."

"Good idea," said Dale. "I'll prepare the paperwork and file it, asking that it be set for hearing at an early date. There is little to be gained by delaying this thing."

The motion was filed and on the hearing date, granted, there having been no objection from the county attorney.

Pedro was examined, and within two weeks Dale and I got the doctor's written report of his findings, as follows:

> "A 50-year-old Hispanic male presents on June 15, 1964, alleged to have stabbed and killed his 18-year-old daughter. Patient relates to having consumed alcohol in increasing quantities since being injured while working as an underground miner four years ago. Evidence of a fractured left leg is present, causing pain to the patient, who has a pronounced limp which prevents his being able to work.
>
> "His manner of speech, muscle tone and mobility suggest a long history of alcohol consumption. Blood and urine tests reveal an advanced state of liver and kidney disease. Palpation of the liver suggests an advanced case of cirrhosis of the liver. Patient has a life expectancy of one-and-one-half to two years with complete abstention from alcohol consumption. (signed) E.B. Jolley, M.D."

This was not good news for Pedro, but at least it gave us a shot at keeping Cruz out of the gas chamber.

In the meantime, Dale and I learned that the county attorney had photos of the victim. Upon request, copies of the pictures were given to us. They showed the naked body of a full-sized woman lying on the coroner's slab with a large incision under the left breast – a truly graphic photo of the attractive, but very dead, young woman.

We learned from the county attorney that Cruz, his wife Petra, and beautiful 18-year-old daughter, Inez, lived in a small frame house on Brewery Gulch, not one of Bisbee's most glamorous neighborhoods.

Dale and I took Mrs. Cruz' deposition and learned that Pedro had been addicted to strong drink for a number of years and his drinking became increasingly worse since his injuries of years ago. She told us that their daughter, Inez, was a senior at Bisbee High School, and an honor student. She was outgoing and popular – indeed, secretary of her class.

Mrs. Cruz related that for several weeks Pedro had been accusing her of being pregnant by another man, and that she and Pedro had not had sexual intercourse because he could not perform due to his injury and alcoholic condition.

Mrs. Cruz was 45 and, like some women her age, had become heavy and had developed a large belly, suggesting pregnancy. Pedro, in his drunken stupor, had convinced himself that she was pregnant, and he knew that he could not be the father of the child.

Argument followed argument. Pedro sat on the small porch of his Brewery Gulch home for two weeks prior to the murder sharpening a large butcher knife to a razor's edge.

Finally, on a Sunday morning, Pedro, as usual, accused Petra of infidelity and again asserted that she was pregnant. Petra, of course, denied this, and a violent argument followed. Inez, who was on the porch with her parents, begged them to stop arguing.

Finally, Cruz said, "I am going to prove once and for all that you are pregnant," and lunged at Petra to cut open her stomach to reveal the imagined child. Inez jumped in front of her mother to protect her, and Cruz stabbed her in the heart, killing her instantly.

Faced with these facts, Dale and I were in a real quandary. What defense could we present? No question that Cruz had killed his daughter. No question that it was premeditated. The doctor's report had shown that Cruz, although soaked in alcohol, was mentally sane. The physical did reveal, however, that Cruz had an advanced case of cirrhosis of the liver from which he could not recover. The doctor felt that it was progressive and terminal.

The graphic pictures showed Inez laid out in the morgue with a gaping wound from the stabbing as well as the incisions of the medical examiner, which opened the entire chest cavity. They were indeed a set of highly inflammatory photographs. We figured the county attorney could get these pictures before a jury and if this were done, the jury would tear off the door of the jury room to return a guilty verdict of premeditated murder in the first degree, punishable by death.

Dale and I figured the best we could do for Pedro was to cop a plea with the county attorney. This we did, in return for pleading Pedro guilty to a lesser degree of murder, still punishable by death, if the judge so decided.

The county attorney agreed to make no recommendation to the judge. In other words, he would not insist on the gas chamber because he knew from the doctor's report that Pedro's time on this earth was limited, and further, the appeals could take years.

With such a plea, the judge could sentence Cruz to death, or to life without parole.

We eloquently argued to Judge William E. Kimble that a life sentence without parole was tantamount to death. The judge bought our recommendation and sentenced Pedro to life imprisonment without parole.

Cruz went to prison in Florence, where he died five months later of cirrhosis of the liver.

A CASE OF FOOT IN MOUTH – 1966

One late afternoon after work in 1966, four of us "gringos" from Douglas left to go to Nacozari, Sonora, for a weekend of fishing.

We all loaded into my Jeep Wagoneer – Bill Gregory, owner of Gregory Florists, a flower shop-nursery; Aaron Loney, publisher of the *Douglas Daily Dispatch*; Sid Moeur, owner of the Hartford Insurance Agency; and I. Having already obtained our immigration visas at the Mexican Consulate in Douglas, we crossed the border at Agua Prieta, where I secured a car permit from Mexican customs. With our tourist visas now stamped, we headed for Nacozari in a jovial mood.

I had made arrangements to use my father's staff house at Nacozari, which he leased from the Moctezuma Copper Company, a Mexican subsidiary of the Phelps Dodge Corporation. The house had cooking and sleeping facilities.

When we reached kilometer 47 on the dirt road 21 miles south of the border, there was an adobe shack with signs out in front which read, *"Obligatorio - Alto"* and then under that *"Aduana."*

As ordered by the signs, we stopped and waited patiently in front of the door. Finally, an unkempt Mexican customs officer came out with his tie loosened and his hair disheveled. Although it was early evening, he had obviously been taking a siesta.

Coming to the driver's side of the car, he said, *"Donde van?"* (Where are you going?)

"We are going to Nacozari." (*Vamos a Nacozari.*)

"*Aver su permiso para el carro.*" (Let me see your car permit.)

I handed him the permit, which he examined carefully. Obviously in a bad mood because we had disturbed his siesta, he said, "*Donde están sus permisos de imigracion?*" (Where are your immigration permits?)

Turning to my colleagues, I said, "He wants to see our immigration visas."

My companions passed their visas to me and I handed them to the officer. He took his time examining them, gave them back to me, and proceeded to walk around the Jeep. Returning to the driver's side, he pointed through the window behind me, and asked, "*Que son esas cosas?*" (What are those things?)

"*Son cañas para pescar.*" (They are fishing rods.)

"Let me see your fishing licenses."

"We don't have any fishing licenses."

"You must have fishing licenses."

I wasn't surprised at this point, because being a customs official and not having anything to do with any enforcement of fishing regulations, he obviously was looking for a *mordida* (an under-the-table monetary tip).

I said, "*Es muy tarde para obtenerlos.*" (It's too late to get them.)

"*Deben regresar a Agua Prieta para obtener licencias de pescar.*" (You will have to go back to Agua Prieta to get fishing licenses.)

I turned to my confused colleagues and said, "This sonovabitch is going to make us go back to Agua Prieta to get fishing licenses!"

At this, the Mexican officer said, in perfect King's English, "Sir, I resent being called a son-of-a-bitch!"

Startled, I asked, "Officer, where did you learn to speak English like that?"

"I was an exchange officer from the Mexican government to the United States Military Academy at West Point."

"You must have done something terrible to be posted here at kilometer 47. There is a federal fishing office in Nacozari, and we will get licenses there."

"If you return this way and I am on duty and you have fish, you are in big trouble if you don't have fishing licenses."

We proceeded to Nacozari, had a wonderful weekend, ate many steaks, drank many highballs and caught many fish.

As we approached kilometer 47 on our way home, we were apprehensive. We stopped, but he had been replaced. Permanently perhaps?

OF MICE AND MAGGOTS – 1967

Horace Davis Post No. 46, the all-black American Legion Post in Douglas, has been active for a number of years, particularly since World War I, when some troopers from two divisions of black soldiers stationed at Fort Huachuca moved to Douglas and founded the post.

One afternoon in April of 1967, my secretary buzzed me on the intercom and said, "Eddie Price is on the line and would like to speak with you."

"Good. Please put him on."

"Mr. Williams, this is Eddie Price, and I'm down at the Horace Davis Post with some friends. We've been drinking soda pops and visiting.

"We ordered our sodas from the bartender, and one of the ladies in our group gagged while drinking hers. She spit out what she hadn't swallowed. It looked like maggots. There were still some in the bottle. She vomited and was really sick. We need to talk to you. Can you see us?"

Always able to handle another client, I said, "Eddie, come by my office and bring the bottle with what's left in it."

A short time later, Eddie and Mrs. Kitty Green arrived and were shown into my office. Eddie was for many years the dogcatcher for the City of Douglas and was well known to me – a clever man, devious at times. A sergeant in the Army when he retired, he moved to Douglas with his wife and family. Eddie also had a wife in Agua Prieta, across the border from Douglas. Sometime during his military career, he had broken his jaw and was unable to chew well or bite down hard. He loved fish and ate all he could get his hands on. My friends and I made many fishing trips to Angostura Dam in Mexico, and Eddie was always waiting for whatever fish we would bring him.

Mrs. Green was an attractive black lady, about 35 years old, well dressed, and well educated. "Mr. Williams," she said, "we were sitting around drinking sodas when I drank part of a bottle at the club. I drank some and spit the rest out. Eddie was there with two other post members. I was very sick and vomited four times. I looked at the bottle and saw the remains of what I had swallowed. It looked like a cluster of maggots. I brought you the bottle with the maggots in it."

I examined the contents of the bottle, and sure enough, there appeared to be maggots in what remained of the cola drink. I said to Eddie, "Go down to the post and ask the bartender to show you the rest of the case, and if you find any contamination in the remaining bottles, buy the entire case and call me."

Eddie left, and about thirty minutes later called to report, "There are three contaminated bottles remaining in the case, along with six that are okay."

I said, "Eddie, take the three contaminated bottles – don't uncap them – along with one that is not contaminated, to the Arizona State Department of Health office on F Avenue. I'll call George Griffin, the health officer, to ask if he can keep them for us."

"Hello, George, this is Ben Williams. I wonder if you'd be so kind as to keep three contaminated soda bottles and an uncontaminated bottle in a safe place. We need to preserve them as evidence in a lawsuit that will undoubtedly be filed."

"Sure, I'll take good care of them. They'll be safe."

Mrs. Green asked, "Will I have a lawsuit?"

"Well, Mrs. Green, I'm convinced you do have a case, but I don't know what it might be worth in damages. We have to show that you were made sick and that there has been an injury to you that can be measured in dollars."

"Mr. Williams, there's no question I was made sick, and I doubt if I can ever drink another soda after this terrible experience."

I took the information needed to prepare a summons and complaint to file in the Superior Court at Bisbee, and was reminded of a case I'd studied at the University of Arizona Law School, which had originated out of the same court.

Frank Thomas, a lawyer practicing law in Bisbee at the time and later elected Superior Court judge, had filed and tried a mouse-in-the-coke-bottle case, a classic case used to teach law school students the principle of *res ipsa loquitur* (the thing speaks for itself).

Frank Thomas filed his case, alleging that on the evening of February 6, 1931, his client purchased a bottle of Coca-Cola which had been bottled by the Cochise Coca-Cola Bottling Works, and that after drinking from the bottle, the plaintiff noticed that it didn't taste right. He looked and discovered the skeleton of a mouse remaining in the bottle. Frank alleged that "as a result of drinking said beverage containing said decayed, putrefied mouse, plaintiff became seriously ill, suffered severe shock to his nervous system, underwent the loss of employment and, at the time of drinking said beverage and for a considerable period of time thereafter, suffered great mental pain and shock to his system in general."

The case was tried by Frank, and although the plaintiff had claimed damages in the sum of $3,000, the jury returned with a verdict in the sum of $1,500. That judgment was appealed to the Arizona Supreme Court, and the Court, holding that the $1,500 judgment in the lower court was proper, affirmed it.

The Court further adopted the doctrine of *res ipsa loquitur* and stated that the negligence doctrine applied where plaintiff proved that the thing was under defendant's management and that it caused such an accident as does not ordinarily happen if proper care is used. Therefore, all the plaintiff had to do was show that the mouse or its skeleton were in the bottle and that the plaintiff had consumed part of the contents and had been made ill therefrom.

Knowing that Frank Thomas was then Superior Court judge and that he would be the one who would hear the case, I went to Bisbee and looked in the records to find the exact complaint he had prepared in his mouse case. I modified the complaint to show "maggots" instead of "mouse" and duly filed it for Mrs. Green. I sued for $10,000. Service of the summons and complaint was made upon the local bottler in Douglas, and within the time allowed for answer, I was contacted by Bill Kimble, a practicing lawyer in Bisbee, who informed me that he represented the bottling company and they were denying any negligence.

I really felt good about my case, however, because I had witnesses, Eddie being one of them, to the fact that Mrs. Green had drunk of the bottle containing the maggots and was made sick; that the remaining contents of the bottle had been preserved; further, that there were three other bottles in the very case from which the maggots came which contained foreign material in unopened bottles. My chain of custody of the bottles of contaminated soda was unbroken, and at the time of trial I would subpoena George Griffin to bring the bottles to court to show the jury the three remaining contaminated bottles. I felt I had a "lead pipe cinch" to recover a judgment.

The case sat on the calendar for some time, and finally I mentioned to Bill that I wanted to move it along and get the matter resolved. I prepared a Certificate of Readiness and a Motion to Set and filed it with the court, asking for a trial date. Bill did not object to fixing a trial date, which was set for 60 days in the future.

I began to prepare my case for trial and in so doing contacted a doctor in Douglas who was well known in the county. I felt he would be a good witness. I asked his opinion as to how sick the consumption of maggots might make a person. He said, "Well, Ben, when you boil it all down, the maggots are nothing more than protein and the body will digest the protein quite readily without any difficulty."

I was not happy with his medical opinion but felt he knew what he was talking about.

I contacted George Griffin by phone. "George, this is Ben Williams, and I am preparing my case for trial in just a few weeks. How are the pop bottles you are keeping as evidence for me?"

"Well, Ben, I was going to call and tell you that I no longer have those bottles."

"What happened to them?"

"Well, somehow the word didn't get to the new janitor about the pop. He was filling in for our regular janitor, who was sick. He found them in the office refrigerator and drank them."

"The hell he did!"

"Yes."

"Did they make him sick?"

"No, they didn't bother him at all."

When I saw Bill Kimble the next Monday in Bisbee at the regular call of the calendar, I said, "Bill, you know, there's not much money involved in this lawsuit, and it could turn out to be a waste of everybody's time for what little money we're fighting over. Why don't you contact your client and see if they will authorize a settlement?"

"Okay. I'll see what they say and let you know."

A couple of days later I got a call from Bill. "The client doesn't feel there is any liability, but I talked them into making an offer of $2,500 to settle this thing."

"Bill, I don't believe that's enough. However, I'll contact my client and see what she says."

Ten minutes after talking to Bill, I had Mrs. Green on the phone. "Mrs. Green, the defendants have offered $2,500 to settle. We don't have any evidence any more. I'm sorry to say that the janitor at the state health offices drank the three contaminated sodas and threw out thc partly empty one you brought me. I strongly recommend that we accept their offer and settle as fast as we can."

Reluctantly she said, "Well, Mr. Williams, you know more about it than I do and I'll be guided by your judgment."

I waited a couple of days before calling Bill so he wouldn't feel that I was overly eager. "Bill, it was really hard to convince my client to accept your offer, but she finally agreed. Let's draw a stipulation for dismissal of the suit, and you can send me a check and release."

"Okay. Done."

ALL THAT GLITTERS…– 1968

In 1968, the City of Douglas Water Department Commissioners: Jack Davis, senior engineer at the Phelps Dodge reduction works; L.R. Acosta, an accountant; and Vic Daniel, owner of Copper Maintenance Company, decided it was time to drill a new well. It was to be located next door to the City Water Department offices in the 300 block of Eleventh Street, not quite a block away from the Gadsden Hotel.

Ordinance Number 97, passed and adopted by the mayor and council in May, 1910, gave the commissioners power to control and manage all matters pertaining to the city water system, so they issued a call for bids, publishing the notice in newspapers and trade journals, and posting it on all area and local bulletin boards.

A crotchety 60-year-old man, Earl Lohn, had the lowest qualifying bid. He brought his well-drilling rig to Douglas from Willcox, set it up and got to work. For several days, residents were fascinated with the heavy equipment, the noise and the progress being made.

One of the most interested onlookers was a retired man of leisure with little to do and even less to gossip about, who made it his business to inspect the site extra-early every morning before Earl arrived, and then kibitz him when he did. He would ask infuriating questions like: "How deep are you? Have you hit hard rock? Caliche? What other strata have you encountered? How many feet did you drill yesterday? How many do you think you will drill today? When will it be finished? How much water will it produce? Will the water be potable?"

The kibitzer finally got Earl's goat. That night when everyone was gone, Earl sprinkled iron pyrite on the sand left after the last discharge from the day's work. When "Nosy"arrived – extra-early as usual – next morning, he discovered the golden flecks glistening in the sunshine.

"Earl, Earl, look what I've found," he said, bursting with excitement when the old man showed up to begin the day's drilling. "What are those bright specks in the sand?"

With a straight face and even greater care, Earl inspected the evidence. "Well, I'll be damned. We must have struck gold!"

Thus, old Nosy proved that common iron pyrite deserves the nickname "fool's gold" because he spent the rest of the day spreading the news all over town, "We've struck gold! We've struck gold!"

BAGGED: ONE JUDGE – 1969

On February 24, 1969, Governor Paul Fannin appointed William E. Kimble judge of the Cochise County Superior Court in Bisbee where he had practiced law for a number of years with the firm of Gentry, McNulty & Kimble. His appointment filled the vacancy created by the untimely death of Frank E. Thomas, caused when he tripped and fell down the stairs at the home of Dr. Jolley, a Bisbee doctor.

Not long after his appointment, Bill called me to say he'd been contacted by Colonel George Thorpe, the Judge Advocate General, who was interested in fostering better relations between the military and their civilian counterparts. He'd asked that my friend, Bill, meet and work with them to that end.

Judge Kimble knew that my family owned the Slaughter Ranch at San Bernardino, and asked if it were possible to arrange a quail hunt. We set the date, and Bill and I met with two bird colonels who drove the 50 miles from Fort Huachuca to the Desert Inn Motel where we had breakfast.

One gentleman, a troop commander, sported a beautiful fowling piece and a Tyrolean hunting hat complete with a colorful pheasant feather.

Because many skilled Austrian gunsmiths were idle after World War II, our government assisted them in the making of exceptional hunting weapons like "Fancy Hat's" finely-crafted, over-and-under, 12-gauge shotgun, inlaid with silver engravings of hunting scenes.

Loading our gear, our guns and ourselves in my Jeep Wagoneer, we headed for the ranch with high hopes, but it turned out to be a disappointing day for quail hunting. There were none to be found, and to make things worse, Fancy Hat was relating endless experiences of hunting tigers in India, lions in Africa, and chamois wherever and whatever they were. The only chamois Bill and I knew anything about were those soft cloths used in car washes for polishing vehicles.

It seemed that we had driven all over the country looking for quail, when, as we drove past Granddad's ranch on the way to the Taylor place, Fancy Hat exclaimed, "Stop! I think I just saw something run into that mesquite thicket."

I jammed on the brakes, and in a cloud of dust, the four of us jumped out with our shotguns. Fancy Hat ran toward the brush, and fired, yelling, "I saw a rabbit," just as the judge yelled, "I've been shot!"

We rushed to Bill, who was holding his belly. There was no sign of blood, but when he lifted his shirt, we found a small round puncture wound made by a single lead pellet.

"Damn! It stings like hell!"

"I'll get the merthiolate," I said, heading back to the Jeep for my ubiquitous first aid kit, only to find the tincture of merthiolate bottle empty.

"We could pour whiskey on it," said one colonel, and although the other opined, "Say, whiskey's an excellent anesthetic as well as a great antiseptic," Bill declined the proposed treatment.

Later, Bill told me privately that at the time of the shooting, he thought it would have been a simple matter for the Army to announce with regret that Judge William E. Kimble had overindulged, become falling-down, snot-flying drunk, and shot himself.

Whiskey having been ruled out, Fancy Hat said, "There's sulfur in motor oil…we should get some off the dipstick to cauterize the wound."

"No, not only no, but hell no!" said Bill. "I'd rather head for home and let a real doctor take a look at it."

A few weeks later I saw Bill in court and asked about his wound.

"It was superficial…Dr. Joe Saba removed the pellet. It was just under the skin. My hunting pal and good friend, Dr. Saba thought it was all hysterically funny…and crankcase oil is a lousy antiseptic…it can cause infections. And by the way, Ben...I don't think I want to try improving relations with the military for a while..."

"Have you heard from Colonel Thorpe?"

"Yeah...he said the general had called the colonels on the carpet and properly dressed them down, saying 'I send you men out as my emissaries to foster better relations with the civil authorities, and what do you do? You shoot the Superior Court Judge in the belly! Great work! A fine display of military marksmanship! So much for the fostering of better relationships!'"

SLAUGHTER'S MODEL T – 1980s

John Slaughter, the famous sheriff of Cochise County, a renowned cattleman-businessman, owned a Model T Ford of 1915 vintage. Although his automobile no longer exists, a similar vehicle is on display in the garage at the Johnson Historical Museum of the Southwest, 15 miles east of Douglas. It is well-kept and in running condition.

On a 49-acre parcel, the museum is the old Slaughter Ranch house as it existed at the turn of the century, and was established for the purpose of creating a working ranch much like the one in the old days. Besides the ranch house, there is an ice house, commissary, bunkhouse, garage and stone granary. There is a five-acre pond fed by artesian, or ever-flowing, springs, a barn, and a 2,000-gallon water tank for domestic use.

In the early 1980s, Douglas, Arizona, and Agua Prieta, Sonora, celebrated the Two Flag Festival. There would be an exchange of arts and crafts, and a display – usually in Douglas at the old city water department building, now called The Little Gallery. Our parade would travel north from Fourth Street to Fifteenth Street along G Avenue, the principal business street. Most of the 13,000 citizens of Douglas would line the streets for the parade, as well as hundreds from Mexico.

On one occasion in the 1980s while I was mayor, my wife Daisy and I were invited to ride in the parade along with our good friends, Luis and Molly Cordoba, the *presidente* of Agua Prieta and his wife.

The 1915 Model T automobile was brought to town for the parade. Molly sat on the front seat with a driver from the Johnson Historical Museum of the Southwest, while Daisy, Luis and I rode in the back.

Although the parade route was only eleven blocks long and the weather hot, we had great fun. However, the motor made so much noise that it was difficult to talk or understand one another, and the "firewall" grew uncomfortably hot, almost to the point of burning the shins of the driver and Molly.

Had John Slaughter been alive, he too would have ridden in the parade, and would have enjoyed it every bit as much as we did.

Parade, riding in 1915 Model T

THE CANANEA HANGING – 1980

When I was elected mayor of Douglas in 1980, there had been a rash of car thefts with the vehicles winding up in Mexico. The lack of cooperation between American and Mexican authorities made their recovery almost impossible, the main reason being that in Mexico, each new *presidente* (mayor) appointed a new chief of police. He in turn appointed new officers, all of whom served at the pleasure of the *presidente*. When his term was over, they all left, so there was a constant turnover of policemen.

Wanting to establish the best relations between Douglas and the Mexican municipalities of Agua Prieta, Nacozari, Cananea, Hermosillo and Nogales, a perfect opportunity arose when a friend and restauranteur died.

For years, Amado and Mercedes Alvarez served the best Mexican food in Douglas at their Coney Island Café on the northeast corner of Eighth Street and G Avenue. Daisy and I had our favorites: she was partial to the chicken *fajitas*, while I liked their *enchiladas "Sonorense"* (flat) with refried *frijoles*.

Except for the space occupied by a one-foot-high, twelve-foot-long, 1920s panoramic photograph of Cananea, a shelf bearing Amado's prized collection of unique whiskey bottles circled the walls of the entire building. Mercedes, who had babysat my sister, Teresa, and me, knew how much I admired the photograph. When Amado died, she came to me to settle her affairs, and insisted I accept it.

Real estate broker, Sid Moeur, the grandson of Dr. Benjamin Baker Moeur,

Governor of Arizona from 1933 to 1937, handled the sale of the business. Sadly, Amado's bottles sold for very little.

Thrilled with Mercedes' gift, I rolled it up and took it to Luis Cordova, owner of a framing shop in Agua Prieta. He was pleased to make the custom frame for me, as well as a copper plaque to attach to the frame which read:

"To the people of Cananea, Sonora
from
Ben F. Williams, Jr.
Mayor of the City of Douglas, Arizona."

I contacted the *presidente* of Cananea and told him my fine, bilingual chief of police, Theo Neilson, and I, would like to personally deliver a gift for his people. He said that Cananea would soon be celebrating Cinco de Mayo with fiestas and parades in which all the children would march wearing their respective school colors. He invited my wife, Daisy, and me, and Police Chief Theo Neilson and his wife, Martha, to be official guests of Cananea, and to sit on the balcony of his office in city hall overlooking the parade route.

Elated, I carefully wrapped the panorama in its elegant new frame, tied it securely to the top of my Jeep Wagoneer, and on the fifth of May, drove the 60 miles to Cananea. We were met at the outskirts of town by a delegation from the *presidente's* office and were escorted to city hall where I presented him with the panorama. We were served lunch in his office and enjoyed the parade from his balcony.

Another delegation, including long-time friend and lawyer, Licenciado Erasmo Lozano Rocha, joined us for the two-block walk to the famous *La Carcel de Cananea* (the jail of Cananea), which had been made into a museum.

The popular Sonoran folksong, "El Corrido de Cananea," was composed by Ruben Fuentes in 1917, and is about a jailed copper miner:

Voy a dar un pormenor
de lo que me ha pasado,
que me han agarrado preso
Siendo un gallo tan jugado."

(I am going to detail what happened to me,
that they have taken me prisoner,
being a well-played rooster –
even though I've been around
and should have known better.)

We enjoyed a lively ceremony and speeches in front of the museum as the panorama was hung. The picture, whose history was so meaningful to me, still hangs inside the museum's main entrance.

On occasion of presentation of panoramic photo of Cananea by author to Mayor and people of Cananea; Cananea Mayor fifth from left; Daisy Williams, wife of author, and author in back row; Martha Neilson; back row, glasses and white hair, Lic. Erasmo Losano Rocha; to his right, Theo Neilson, Chief of Police, Douglas

DUH!

Joe is a cattle rancher. His home is in the Chiricahua Mountains 70 miles southeast of Tucson.

Joe's neighbor, Ralph, is a college professor who recently planted several fruit trees. After he planted them, his water pump broke.

Ralph knew Joe had a water truck so he asked him if he could borrow it to water his trees.

Joe said, "Sure," and showed the professor how to use the tanker.

When Joe finished explaining the system he asked, "Do you have any questions?"

"Yes. How will I know when the tank is empty?"

SERAPE VISA – 1985

When I was practicing law in Douglas in 1985, Joe Rice, a ranching client, came to me and said he needed a bronc-buster for his cattle ranch in Colorado. He wanted someone who had experience with horses and knew how to gentle and break them without breaking their spirit. He had had a lot of success with Mexican cowboys because they seemed to understand livestock, and especially horses, very well.

Joe had been to the local employment office where they told him there was no one available to do that kind of work around Douglas. He was also told he would have to make an application and publish a want ad. And, after publication in the Douglas newspaper – assuming that there was nobody available for the job – his application would be sent to Phoenix to the employment office for review. If approved in Phoenix, it would be forwarded to San Francisco to the appropriate office for consideration.

We crafted a notice which we published in the *Douglas Daily Dispatch,* advertising for a "horse breaker – male." Joe wanted a cowboy rather than a cowgirl inasmuch as the bronc-buster would have to live with six or seven other cowboys in a common bunkhouse.

Nobody responded to the ad in the Douglas paper, and the application and a copy of the ad were sent to Phoenix for approval. The application was approved in Phoenix and forwarded to the San Francisco office.

In the meantime, Joe had located someone from Mexico to fill the position, but he needed approval in order to get the cowboy a special visa permitting him to come into the United States legally.

San Francisco denied the application and returned it to Joe, stating that the reason for denial was that it was "discriminatory" in that it was an application for a male and should have included a female as well.

All the applications and requirements imposed on Joe in seeking to get approval for his Mexican bronc-buster had taken a considerable amount of time, and Joe's need for a man to break his horses was becoming critical.

When Joe received the denial from San Francisco, he was told that it had to be sent to Washington, D.C. for confirmation before becoming final. He was further told that if he felt there was any basis for appeal of the decision at San Francisco, he could submit an appeal to Washington.

We drafted an appeal which, among other things, stated that it would be awkward for a female bronc-buster to live in the same quarters with the six or seven men sharing all the same facilities, and further, there was only one bunkhouse on the ranch.

While the matter was being considered in Washington, I received a telephone call one morning from Joe, who informed me that he was in trouble. The call came from El Paso, and Joe told me he was allowed only a certain amount of time for his call. He related that he was in jail, having been arrested by the border patrol at Truth or Consequences, New Mexico, the night before, and had been brought, along with Juan Lopez, to the El Paso detention center.

I asked Joe if he was in a place where he could speak freely.

"Yes."

"All right, tell me the story."

Joe related that he had taken the Mexican cowboy from Sonora with him in his pickup truck from Douglas and was on his way to Colorado when they approached the border patrol checkpoint at Truth or Consequences about nine o'clock at night. He was too close to the checkpoint to turn around and backtrack, and had no recourse but to proceed to the checkpoint. He told Juan Lopez, the cowboy, to throw a serape over his head, to sit quietly in the cab, and to say nothing.

When Joe pulled up and stopped, as was required, a border patrol officer asked if he were a U.S. citizen. He responded that he was. The officer then asked, "Who's that?"

"Oh, that's my mother-in-law and she's very sick."

Whereupon, the border patrol officer said, "Well, by golly, you're in luck because we happen to have a fine nurse inside who can help your mother-in-law. Let's get her into the station where she can be examined."

Of course, at this point the jig was up and Joe and Juan were arrested. Joe asked if I could help. I told him I had a good friend who was a lawyer in El Paso who had worked with me in the past and had achieved excellent results. Giving Joe the lawyer's name and telephone number, I said I would also call to pave the way for him.

The lawyer in El Paso was able to obtain Joe's release upon payment of a fine. Juan Lopez was deported.

A few weeks later, we received notice from Washington that our appeal had been successful based on "humanitarian reasons."

Joe never told me what the ultimate outcome was, or whether or not he was able to "import" another bronc-buster for his Colorado ranch.

Oftentimes our government, in an effort to be helpful, does little more than screw up the works to the detriment of citizens who want to comply with the law, but for one (political?) reason or another (red tape?) find it difficult to do so.

ARIZONA PIONEER

While I was fishing in Arizona with my son recently, he suggested that I look into whether or not I was eligible for a "Pioneer" hunting and fishing license. These are issued to folks over 70 years of age who have been a resident in Arizona for a minimum of 25 years.

Upon presenting myself to the Fish and Game Department's office in Tucson, I said to the officious lady at the counter, "I would like to get a Pioneer hunting and fishing license. What are the requirements?"

"You must have resided in the state of Arizona for more than 25 years and you must be at least 70 years old or older. How long have you resided in Arizona?" she snapped.

"I've lived here 75 years."

"Are you 70 years old or older?"

Hearing a sudden guffawing from the other license applicants at the counter, it dawned on her that I was more than eligible.

She issued my Pioneer hunting and fishing license forthwith.

Printed in the United States
92191LV00002B/175-400/A